THE KINDRED PROJECT

Vol. II

A collaborative collection of poetry and prose

by

J. Raymond

J. Raymond

1

THE KINDRED PROJECT

WRITTEN BY J. RAYMOND

Cover Design by Mitch Green

FIRST EDITION
COPYRIGHT 2024 © J. RAYMOND
WWW.JRAYMONDWRITING.COM

DEDICATION

To the grief stricken and lonely.
To the downtrodden and exhausted.
To the addicts
and those fighting to break the cycle.
To those who've been left for dead.
To those who had to leave to live.

To the lovers all alone.
To those still finding their way home.
To the musicians.
To the mothers.
To the fathers.
To those called upon
to raise sons and daughters.

To anyone starting over,
again.
To anyone searching for answers.
To the runners.
To the empaths.
To the healers and outcasts.

To you.
To us.
To all.

PREFACE

When writing a book, themes seem to surface on their own. Almost subconsciously. I've never been one to force a metaphor. The more I allow each poem to flow, the better. Oftentimes, the direction I set off in at the beginning of a piece will wind up taking me somewhere completely unexpected. The end result required space and time to be fleshed out naturally.

For example, I sat down to type the preface to this book, from my couch. Hunched over, with my laptop open atop my ottoman. My back aches. It's uncomfortable. Right beside me, my two-month-old daughter stirs in her sleep, and I can't help but stop and stare. She just might be the most perfect thing I've ever known. My life is nothing like what I had imagined only a few years ago.

When I began working on the first volume of The Kindred Project, in 2022, I was in the very early stages of recovery. My alcoholism and drug abuse had essentially destroyed my life, and I was starting over, from absolute rock bottom, with nothing to my name. Nothing, that is, except hope. For the first time in nearly a decade, I knew I wanted to live. And I wanted desperately to connect with others. The conversations and stories from that first book, in many ways, kept me afloat during one of my most challenging chapters.

Shortly after releasing TKP, I was inundated with messages and emails from individuals all around the world, asking if I would turn their story into poetry. So, I, once again, announced that I was looking for 115 brave souls who would be willing to connect with me, and immediately began work on volume two. My life was gradually getting back on track (I even owned furniture again!), and throwing myself into the creative process seemed to be the safe, obvious move.

Then, when I wasn't ready or expecting it, love arrived. Funny how that happens, huh? I met someone who showed me why everything before her had to fail. Someone who settled my spasmodic spirit. Someone who showed me I'm so much more than the worst versions of myself. Turns out you don't need to be completely whole or healed before falling in love. In fact, since nearly no person is completely whole or healed, I'd strongly recommend finding someone you can grow and heal alongside. Someone willing to work with you, hand-in-hand.

Within a year, we were married and expecting.

My friends, life truly does come at you fast. Rushing in whether you're prepared or not. And whatever idea you may be holding onto of what your future should look like, is practically meaningless. So, believe whatever you'd like. Fate follows its own path. Destiny is designed on its own timeline. Blessings arrive regardless of your plan. Stay open. Be somewhere beautiful things have a chance to thrive.

As I began interviewing contributors for volume two, I was quickly reminded of just how resilient we all are. We overcome impossible odds. The stories shared with me were inspiring, of course. But more than that, they served as proof of how any one of us can change the trajectory of our entire life. We can outgrow what's no longer meant for us. We can rebuild and recreate our own futures.

While editing, I began to notice a few themes unknowingly repeated throughout the book....

You'll read of gardens. Places we grow out of. But also places we remove roots and weeds from.

You'll read of oceans. Something so powerful we can be crushed by it. Yet, something we can just as easily float and drift atop.

You'll read of honoring the different versions of oneself. Perhaps the most prominent underlying message I garnered from my interviews. We are (hopefully) not merely one thing. We evolve. We change. Throughout the course of our lives, we will become variants of the person we were previously. Shedding and rendering. Reforming and adapting. A never-ending before and after example.

You'll read of breaking. To me, this is the pre-requisite to most anything worthwhile. The amazing contributors I had the privilege of speaking with had stories replete with hardships. Abuse. Addiction. Failing. Death. Heartbreak. Grief. Illness. And despite their tragedies, they endured. With the same hope and optimism that I, myself, stubbornly clung to years ago.

And you'll read of perseverance. This was the one word I used to describe volume one. It's the word I would use again here. We persevere. We fight. We survive.

A HUGE THANK YOU to the 115 of you who opened their hearts, confided in me, and then trusted me enough to make art with their pieces. I'm honored and humbled to share your stories with the world.

I hope these words reach you and resonate.

THE KINDRED PROJECT

Vol. II

A collaborative collection of poetry and prose

by

J. Raymond

J. Raymond

Wild Imperfections

My hope is that you feel safe with me.

That you feel free to be all those strange,
quirky versions of yourself you've kept hidden
and buried down deep.
I know how hard it is for some of us
simply to exist softly.
To be gentle in a world
that's been everything but
towards us.
My hope is that you know it's ok to be disheveled and confused.
It's ok to be afraid.
It's ok if the only pieces you bring me
are the ones you're not sure what to do with.
My hope is that maybe together
we can reassemble one another better.
Don't posture.
Please, don't come to me artificially.
I know how it feels to fall short of expectations
you never even set for yourself.
My spirit learned to undress itself in the dark,
and redress itself to suit their liking,
to fit their needs.
I prefer us both naked and exposed.
My hope is that when you see me,
you feel at home.
Check your pretensions at the door.
Bring your wild imperfections.
Because here,
everyone "out of place"
no longer is.

Right Time Type

I like people with urgency.
With eyes the color of excitement.
You see it when they speak about their passions
and dreams.

I like
  right-now-is-the-right-time
    type of people.
Who aren't waiting on stars to align.
They're going to tell you how they feel
because they know the heavy weight
of words unspoken.
I like people who have seen and survived tragic things.
They carry a quiet strength that's reassuring.
You see it in the way they listen.
Like they, too, know death.
  They, too,
can relate to the way pain lingers on
long after the person who caused it is gone.
I like people who no longer cover up their smiles,
who've got a few hairs out of place.
Who laugh and dance and sing as if the world *is* watching.
The ones who aren't afraid to let me know when I'm wrong.
The ones who'll love me through my worst seasons
and celebrate alongside me come spring.
I'm tired of wasting time on timidity
and half-stepping my way through life.
I want to run alongside people whose souls are starved
for everything life has in store for us.
I want every moment *made* for us.
Every moment *meant* for us.
We are in the right place at the right time.
Let's not keep our dreams waiting any longer.

So Much So

My problem is I love things with such ferocity
they become a part of me.

There are no shady parts of my heart.
It's all ablaze.
It's all wild.
That's not something I'm ashamed of anymore.

When I look in the mirror,
I see someone both humbled and proud.
Someone who took the knives in their back
and made them bladed wings.
Someone who freely extends the hand
they once needed.
Someone who knows that laughter
is the true luxury of life.
Someone who quit seeking pity
and stopped feeling sorry for themselves.
Someone whose crooked, imperfect smile
was earned the hardest ways imaginable.
Someone who still speaks kindly about those hoping
they come undone.
Someone who will never, ever give up
on those closest.

My problem is that I'm so loyal
a broken heart has become customary.
My problem is that I continue to expect people
incapable of loving themselves properly,
to love me in all the ways I know damn well
I deserve.
It took me my entire life,
but when I look in the mirror,
I finally love all the things I see -
so much so, they became all of me.

You Would, Too

I should know better than to boast,
because I know how abruptly a world can be turned upside down.
I know well how a day, a moment, a snap-second instant,
   can break you in half.
But there's sunlight erupting out of my chest,
and gratitude flying out from its cage.
My spirit,
it seems, can't be contained.
My heart,
just won't beat quietly.
I can't help but fly higher and higher,
to shout into the clouds,
to sing to the heavens,
to let my joy rain down.
Because I know...
I swear to you I know
what being buried alive feels like.
If you knew the price I paid to reach the peace I feel today,
you would sing too.
And that's my hope for you -
for us.
That we turn our tragedies into something which moves the world.
Into something we're not afraid to boast over.
We'll use the heavy weight of heartache
as reasons to live massively loving lives.
I've sat in shame and sadness,
   so now I stand proudly,
and with enough light that it reaches others easily.

If you knew the price I paid to be here today,
   you'd be shining, too.

Let This Be

Not much matters until the work begins.
Real love is what takes place
   once *easy* is over.
When a feeling requires action.
Growth demands that we sacrifice.

Where we go from here
   is entirely up to us.
Together forever
   was never guaranteed.

Hear me when I say,
I still want the world for you and I.
There's no future I can imagine
that you're not in.

But I'm worried.
I feel us unraveling, fraying,
tearing at the seams.
I think we're sinking.
I feel us falling.
Don't you see what's happening?
Somewhere along the way, we split off in different directions.
Now we're at a crossroads.
We've lost our way home.
Maybe this was what was meant to be.
Maybe this is where we'll find our strength.
Please,
let this be where we learn our resiliency.

Delicate & Relentless

I'd like to say that regardless of who I'm with,
my light shines brightly.
But that's not necessarily the case.
Not everybody brings out the best of me.
There are parts I keep hidden unknowingly.
But every so often, someone unexpected will come crashing into me.
They tap into promise and passion
I wasn't even sure still existed.

This is why if I cannot grow with you,
I refuse to settle for you.

Understand this – I don't need anyone to make me happy.
I am dependent on myself today.
I take my life, my love, my time and energy
seriously.
So, if you hear from me,
if I'm giving you pieces normally kept safely inside myself,
it's because I truly want to.

My love isn't any more valuable than the next person's,
I know that.
Yet, it's all I have.
It's priceless.
Delicate and relentless.
Please respect it. Please receive it.
Please realize that what we're doing here together
is sacred to me.
This is why anything one-sided or unreciprocated
will always be unacceptable.

Simply put,
I refuse to grow roots in neglected gardens.

In Hand

The only thing that matters is now.
It's all we have in hand.
We hold and give away our presence,
hoping only that it's cherished.
Treated with the love and respect our moments deserve.

I think of all that had to transpire
simply for us to exist.
What it took for our paths to cross.
It's practically miraculous.
And regardless of our time together,
that will always be true.
We are two shooting stars impossibly colliding.
And yet,
I accept that nothing is guaranteed.
Nothing is promised,
other than the parts of you I'll now carry with me.
You'll always occupy my heart.
Taking up space somewhere very few others will ever see.
A place I don't show many.
And whether the story of us is just beginning
or coming to an end,
I won't allow it to affect the words I'm writing.
It won't change the way I feel for you.
And right now -
  we are the only thing that matters.

Foyer Mirrors

And from now on
I'm going to be everything I've needed from others.

I'll be kind to myself on days I'm down for no good reason.
I'll stop being pulled out of my own humanness, and simply accept it.
I'll give myself space to be childish and immature
without judgement or advice.
I'll show up.
I'll stay,
walk quietly beside myself.
I'll listen without responding.
I'll sit with grief and keep myself company.
I'll help myself back up
when I stumble unexpectedly
and remind myself that it's ok to fall.
We all do it.
No need to be ashamed or embarrassed.
I'll forgive myself more quickly, more easily,
and never hold my faults overhead as leverage.
I'll celebrate little victories
without the need of anybody's approval.
When I fail,
I'll remind myself that coming up short
still puts me further ahead than I was.
I'll be compassionate to myself on the days I'm heavy-hearted.
Encouraging whenever I'm filled with worry and doubt.
Patient on ill-tempered days
and gentle on the hardest ones.

One of the most important lessons I've learned is
the way I deserve to be treated is always my responsibility.
I can only blame others so much
for what I allow.
All the beauty and love in my life will not cease
simply because someone withholds theirs from me.

Whoever We Decide

We must embrace our breaking.
Don't resist the hardships.
Everything we are experiencing is a lesson.
Lean into it.
Learn to love where growth comes from.
Our struggles will one day be examples -
    something we can pull strength from and say,
    with confidence,

I've been through worse. I will survive this.
This will not be the death of me.
I'm not finished yet.

Being afraid of the unknown is no reason to run and hide.
Who we become
will be because of what we overcome.
Those never battle tested
are never ready for war.
The ones never contested
can never be reinforced.

Something beautiful happens to a spirit
that stands back up
after the storms subside -
The very same places instilling fear in some
create bravery in others.
It's up to us.
Who we are
    is whoever we decide.

Wildfires

For now, let's leave these emotions unspoken.
Just long enough to be certain that what we're feeling
is real.
Those three little words weigh tons.
We keep them buried beneath fears and old wounds.
Wearing our scars openly,
   proudly -
evidence of our resilience.

Lay your hand on mine.
Touch me everywhere I've been hurt before.
Feel it...
   here.
The way it healed took years.
The price to move on
   was paid in long nights and heavy tears.

Forgive me for moving slowly.
I still remember what it's like to be broken.

There are still pieces of me missing.

So, for now,
let's save some of the fire for ourselves.
And grow warmer from the inside out.

What's important is not how intensely love arrives,
   but how long we keep it burning.

Unpalatable

For most of my life I've been told to be
and do
the opposite.
Be someone other than who I am.
When it rained,
I was told to beam like sunshine.
When I finally found my confidence,
I was told to sit quietly.
Then,
once my pride was stripped again,
they asked why I wasn't smiling.

My happiness has offended you.
My depression has made you uncomfortable.
My peace upset those suffering.
My suffering agitated the privileged.
When I was starving
the world fed me lessons,
only to tax me once full.

Since it's all the same to you,
I'll just be me. Flawed, exposed, humbled, proud.
And for reasons I'll never care to understand,
that will bother some.

Just keep your hands off my heart.

For most of my life
I've been chastised and criticized
for being the only person I know how to be.
I've exhausted myself, attempting to be who or what you want.
Extinguished my own fire,
worried I might burn someone who prefers me cold.
Nobody will bleed or grieve or feel
the things I stow within.
And no longer will I keep them imprisoned...
Clutch your fucking pearls.
I don't care,

I'm not carrying your baggage.
There's a bitter taste in my mouth,
left behind from biting my tongue.
Now,
I'll press my lips to the sweetness that my life finally is,
with zero interest in your palate.
My peace is so valuable,
   I can't afford to entertain your disdain.

We live in a world where people who are filled with love
aren't sure how to show it,
and the ones filled with hate
can't contain it.

Practically Miraculous

Something magical,
practically miraculous,
happens once you're aware of everything you are.
The heavy, rotting parts no longer serving you
break free.

My greatest gift to you
will be the time given to you, when needed.
And the time I give you back,
once it no longer is.

Being alone is no longer a hardship.
My own company is not a detriment.
It took years of peeling back the layers of my heart
to find who I truly am at its core.
And maybe that's what excites me most these days –
knowing my own strength.
There's tremendous peace found in perseverance.
The list of things I thought I'd never overcome is long.
The horrors and heartbreak I've outrun
took me somewhere abundant
where love grows wildly.
Every person I allowed to touch me deeply
helped uncover parts of myself I'm proud of.
Parts I used to build a wall around myself.
Not to hide behind – but to sit atop,
alongside those these views were meant for.

The same sun rising,
is setting for some.
And I've learned to be grateful for the lessons each brings me.

Shifting Senses

My voice is changing, and I like the way it sounds.
There's volume and defiance in it.
And weight.
More truth and conviction than before.
Loving words no longer stuck in my throat,
set free like sparrows.
The songs I'm singing aren't for everybody.
I think I like that, too.

My vision is changing, and I like what I'm seeing.
There's a focus and acuity to it.
And color.
And recognition of the things awaiting me.
And acceptance of things no longer smiling back in my direction.

Where there was once fear and anger,
grows courage and forgiveness.
My world is changing.
My life is changing.
And I'm not entirely sure if it's because of me,
or for me,
or some combination of both, maybe.
But what I know for certain is that it wasn't always this beautiful here.
I've come a long way to find some place safe.
My senses, heightened.
My heart, full.
My door, open.
And please,
make yourself at home.
Everything I earned, I earned for us.

All My Love

Don't confuse my acceptance
with indifference.
I let everything breathe,
knowing fate isn't something to be forced.
I let everything be,
knowing what's intended needs no remorse.

Not everyone will understand,
but I'm still learning to believe that I'm deserving of good things.
Finding trust in optimism without entitlement.

There's a lot of upside to me today.
Don't confuse my confidence with arrogance.
I'm just growing.
I'm just soaring.
If you knew how far I'd come you'd be proud of me, too.
Beautiful things might be fleeting.
Let's appreciate them while we can.
Don't hate the changing seasons.
Let's enjoy the blue skies while they last.
I let everyone run,
knowing their journey is forever their own.
I let everyone wander,
knowing what's meant for me
always finds its way home.

I've spent so much time fighting for things meant to leave,
when all along
I should have been fighting for me.
The world gave me every reason to hate,
and still,
   all it gets is all my love.

Forgive Me

Forgive my rough edges.
Forgive the way my heart has hardened.
All I've ever been shown is that softness is perceived
as weakness.
My vulnerabilities -
something to sharpen teeth against.
I've watched my fears come to fruition
in the very same hands that once held me tightly.
Listened to sad songs drip from the lips
of those who promised me forever.

Forgive my distance.
Forgive me for flinching.
Forgive me for protecting myself.
I'm still recovering from all the damage love left behind.
"Trust me" has been strummed on my heartstrings so many times
they've become cutthroat lullabies.
Forgive me for questioning your intentions.
My coping mechanisms are deep seated.
So much of the kindness I know was conditional.
The ones who cut me left before I could stop the bleeding,
so now I just do so openly.
Honestly.

Forgive me.

Not One Thing

What if the reason all the love I've known has failed
is because I continue dragging people into places
meant only for me?

It's grown difficult to give myself to others.
Maybe there's less to give.
Or,
maybe I'm just keeping more to myself now.
I've lost count of how many worst-case scenarios
I've already survived.
Now there's not one thing anyone can tell me
that's more vicious
than the things I've told myself.

I've been abandoned at the ends of the earth
I went to for others.

Maybe all along I should've been carving out a space of my own.
Building myself a comfortable home to keep warm within.
Somewhere safe,
where only my dreams stir me awake,
and everything I find beautiful haunts me.

What if the reason for this season
is that I might finally give myself
everything you never could?

War-Cry

What more will it take for you to respect your strength?
How much heartbreak must you endure before you grasp that fact?

You are beautiful in unseen ways.
Ways requiring time and trust.
Ways not everybody will see.
Keep your heart, mind, and eyes open wide.
Allow doors, chapters, and seasons to close.
You are worthy of nurturing.
You deserve reassurance.
And you are not the tragedies you've experienced.
  You are a miracle already.

The odds of you making it this far,
having overcome every obstacle intended for you, is your war-cry.
You are living proof that something beautiful can grow in the dark.
You are evidence of what's possible when you step into your own light.
Even on the days you fall, fail, break down and feel weak –
you are heroic.
You get back up and learn to laugh again.
You find little glimmers of love in places often overlooked.
You forgive those you believed you never could
and swear to yourself that the days of accepting less than you truly deserve
are over.

Sometimes the light you shine is how you find your way out.
Sometimes, it's how others find their way in.

Show yourself grace for all the ways you learned to grow.
Look at how far you've come....
Be proud of who you are,
and loving
to who you're becoming.

Swimming In Sunshine

You taught me new ways to hurt.
Took my dream come true and made me a fool.
There's no going back to what was.
Deceit this deep
sticks to your psyche.
Drapes a gray veil over a world once bursting with color.
All I see is a version of you
who believed destroying me
was justified.
All I hear are well-spun lies you thought
I deserved to sleep beside.

It's jarring how careless someone can be
with another's heart.
The way the same arms holding you
will break you,
then apologize for the pain they may have caused.

I don't need your remorse.
I needed your loyalty.
I needed your promises kept.
I needed you to hold steady.
Instead, your weakness became my strength.
Your spinelessness made me courageous.
Everything I surrendered freely has now returned to me.
I won't live with the burdens you earned.
I won't blame myself, or label myself naïve.

It's true, you taught me new ways to hurt.
But you also revealed I'm stronger than I realized.
My only mistake was envisioning a future with someone
I'm better off without.
Whenever I cross your mind,
just know that I'm somewhere colors don't fade.
Swimming in sunshine,
and not thinking of you at all.

In The End

We like to act as if we can prepare for miracles.
Yet,
every instance of love I've ever known
came barreling towards me out of nowhere.
Unplanned.
Unsuspected.
Jolting.

The same holds true for hardships.
One moment I'm daydreaming,
and the next I'm navigating, ill-prepared
through a nightmare.
I've never once been ready for a lightning strike.
We open ourselves up, shut ourselves off,
focus on life, our careers, our goals and future,
while the Gods laugh at our best intentions.
Fate deals hands we have no choice but to play.

That person who didn't exist in your world yesterday,
lays their hands on your heart so perfectly today.
Goes and makes music of the noise in your head
and you just fall.
You've found happily ever after...
Until the threat of ending arrives, again, unexpected.
Our armor starts falling apart.
We're not invincible.
We were never forever.
What we once believed would be a love story for the ages,
is reduced to nothing more than a few yellowing pages.

The timing is always right, even when it's wrong.
Because in the end, all we'll have,
is what we had.

Settle For More

Here's the thing about me –
  I absolutely won't settle.

When someone suggests lowering my expectations,
I figure they must not know what having nothing feels like.
My dreams are too vivacious.
They're claustrophobic and never sit still.
Complacency and small-mindedness
don't make for good company.
So, I only set myself free around other dreamers.
People whose imaginations and aspirations play well with mine.
My dreams want to sing and run wild.
They love audacity.
They won't wait.
They won't tone it down.

And my heart is even more ambitious.
More enthusiastic. More on fire.
It's taken me a lifetime to learn to trust it.
To listen to it. To follow it.
I can no longer afford to ignore it.
My heart has bent and yielded to undeserving lovers,
and now wears the scars to prove it.

There's no part of dying alone that scares me,
because I've already lived alongside people
who've made me feel that way.
When you're proud of who you're becoming,
I promise,
choosing yourself
is never settling.

The Bully

Somewhere along the way someone convinced me
my best wasn't good enough.
So, I stopped trying to win and found peace in defeat.
I learned how to bleed.
And when I thought life was through teaching me lessons,
it showed me there's no limit to suffering.
It extends out beyond the horizon – further than you can run.
It reaches down deep.
It laughs when you weep, when you scream,
when you're silent, even.
You discover a level of despair so low
you have no choice but to isolate.

So much of myself needed untangling.

How could anyone treat me with love and decency,
while I'm busy bullying myself?
Anything admirable was undermined,
punched down into the dirt.
But maybe the filthy grit of my heart
is something to be proud of.
Nothing scares me now. Not even people.
I shrug my shoulders over things that send others into a panic.
Somewhere along the way,
I started winning again.
And I noticed that much of the world around me
is so worried about losing,
they don't even try.
They're so afraid of a bloody lip they don't fight for anything.
All I've ever done is fight. For everything.
You know how hard it is to beat someone who isn't afraid to lose?
Maybe that's something to be proud of.
I took my licks and lost plenty.
But I'd still rather feel defeated being myself,
than success as someone else.

Over My Shoulder

You know everything and nothing about me.
You know my past, my secrets.
But not my present.
You exist only over my shoulder.
The only time I see you is while looking backwards.
You were who I needed to leave behind
in order to move forward.

Tell everyone who you believe me to be.
Today, the love I'm given
lays paper-thin kisses against my neck, soft as linen.
It whispers words of assurance.
Looks me in the eyes when telling me that my love
is more than enough.
You nearly had me convinced I would never be happy.
You worked so hard making me think so little of myself.
I thought nobody would want me.

Freedom, the most I've ever known,
happened the moment I stopped living and dying by your opinions.
When I stopped allowing your attitude to alter my own.
I was fighting for the attention of someone who has no clue
who they are.
You spend so much time appeasing the world around you,
that the one within you is a dead thing.
Something rotting.

I don't look over my shoulder anymore.
Freedom, the most I've ever known,
happened the moment I stopped waiting for you to see
how great I could be,
and started being those things solely for me.
It took everything I had to rebuild.
I can no longer afford to fall apart
attempting to make another whole.

Inexplicably

Most love is a temporary experience,
even if the feeling itself is everlasting.
It's difficult to watch a once fiery love
succumb to a slow, phlegmatic death for no reason.
No hatred.
No lying.
No glass breaking or doors hanging off hinges.
Inexplicably,
wide-open skies become low-hanging ceilings.
We bump up against it,
wondering what's stopping us from growing as planned.

You're not my person.
And I'm not your person.
Anymore.

If ever I'm asked about you,
I'll say we were just two people whose intentions outweighed our abilities.
What was once promising and bursting at the seams,
now lies deflated at our feet.

Sometimes the best thing we can do for one another
is what's painful.
Over time, harsh truths lose their sting.
The only thing more obvious than loving the person you see forever in,
is leaving them the second you no longer do.

I've finally reached the point in life where I know
believing in something doesn't make it true.
Being open to love is as much about letting go and setting things free,
as it is about attracting it.

Space is made in absence.
And love finds its way.

All Roses

As I get older,
I wonder whether less is required for happiness,
or if I'm just noticing it in all the places
I once overlooked.

My peace is unassuming.
So modest in its trappings.
I'm constantly awed by the amount of beauty
life squeezes into simplicity.
Humble gifts.
Tiny little treasures.

The late afternoon sun sends golden beams through branches.
I stop,
and let blades of light cut me in half.
Standing still is my thrill.
I'm no longer fast-forwarding through each day,
cherry-picking the best parts of life.

I pause,
then peace plucks the strings of my heart
like a harp.
I swear,
this whole damn thing is musical.
If only I remember to turn the noise down.
I swear,
this whole damn thing is a miracle.
If only I remember to slow down.

Some will go everywhere
and see nothing.
While others go nowhere
and see the whole world.

Spill Your Guts

Don't hide your hot-blooded side.
I want your wildfires.
Impassioned people move me.
Bring your vehemence.
Step on a few toes. Spill your guts across the floor.
Ruffle feathers. Stir birds from branches when you sing.
There's a symphony inside you.
Let us hear the crashing cymbals of your heart.
Upset the easily offended.
Be outrageous.

When our passions don't align exactly,
let us argue our points proudly, passionately.
Let's disagree like two adults who can respect one another
despite our dissent.
If your only identifier is a political party,
let's just remain strangers.
I couldn't possibly care less which side you stand on.

Tell me why you're proud of your children,
and what your last meal would be.
Tell me about the one who got away,
and the last time you cried tears of pure joy.
Tell me who you wish you could see one more time,
and what you'd want them to know.
Tell me what you hope your legacy will be,
and if you talk to God still.

We're so busy showing the world our teeth
that we hardly recognize a smile.
I think it's tragic that the only passion some know
comes from a place of hate.
Instead, take me to every place you love
more than life itself.

Gradient Waves

You're a serotonin shock to my system.
Something too beautiful to break,
too real to hate.
I feel you in my veins.
Coursing through me electrically.
Bringing light into places I wasn't ready to show anybody.
I see you.
Can you see me?

Tell me all you've ever loved, feared, left,
and can't help but think about.
We've been here before and swore
it would be a long time before we fell again.
So, let's love gradually.
Intentionally, like the tide rising.
Let's take our time and make the most of our moment.
I want to float slowly with you.
Ride these rolling waves with you.
Just drift with you.

You're so beautiful, you belong in a museum.
Like artwork I can't help but admire.
I'm sorry for staring.
If you saw yourself the way I do,
you would, too.
They don't make them like you anymore.
This doesn't happen but a few times
in a lifetime.

I've seen these clouds before,
so I spend some time each day putting my feet back on the ground.
If any part of my heart was closed off,
you opened it with ease.
If we never become more than we are right now,
you'll have made me a better person.
A more hopeful person.
And hope is such a beautiful gift to give somebody who only knows hurt.
My heartbeat tick, tick, ticks quicker with your touch.
Until everything you are
disarms everything I used to be.

Catch It

Maybe what makes it all so disappointing,
so underwhelming,
is how we continue to expect the next love we experience
to surpass the greatest love we've ever known.
But...maybe we should.
Maybe it's fair to apply pressure.
To expect something worthy of our entire life.

When I say you're all I want,
what I mean is that I'm blind to everyone who isn't you.
I'm not proud to admit this,
but I hurt a few along the way to you.
I figured heartache was the price paid for temporary love.
Now, I can't even stomach the thought.
My world slows down for you.
Makes room for truth.
You're the first thing I've ever wanted to savor.
To protect.
To nourish and learn.

I wipe infatuation from my eyes,
just to make sure that everything I see isn't a lie.
Your smile sends me messages that sound like safety.
Like I'm accepted.
It's true what they say,
love isn't something you can chase down.
It's something you attract.
All this time I was being disappointed by people
who were never meant for me.
I didn't understand that I was learning to be someone deserving of love.
Deserving of a world I'd sooner give to you
than keep for myself.
These days, I don't have to hold my breath.
Only catch it.

Fists Unfurled

I used to believe that being a man meant you had to be dangerous.
Something rabid and threatening.
A snarling dog without leash.

I thought the number of bottles broken over skulls
 and notches on my bed post
were what mattered most.

As a man,
I'm meant to catch the bullet between my teeth.
Show no fear. Drive fast. Break hearts.
Run with the devil. Don't look back.
Shed no tears.
When you're hurting,
just rub some dirt on it.
Man up. Knuckle up. Sack up. Toughen up.

I did all these things, and I did them well.
But that isn't what makes a man.
Those things aren't courageous.
We're told to be hardened so often
that we don't realize how brave it is to soften.
To be forgiving.
To speak sweetly.
To write a love letter.
To risk it all on a dream that nobody understands.
To follow your heart.
To weep over a lowering casket,
not giving a damn how it's perceived.

I'm more of a man today
because of my gentility.
Because I stopped being too stubborn
to be weak
and admitted I needed help.
I've been so reckless with my life,

believing it to be some hair-raising,
fist-fighting adventure.
But I was only running scared of myself.
Now my fists are unfurled.
My knuckles, no longer bloody.
And I'm not too proud to tell you I love you.
I'm not ashamed of my passions.
I went to the harshest lengths
only to learn that
sensitivity is my greatest strength.

Dead Weight

All you have to do is be you, and I fall.
Like dead weight.
Only, I've never felt more alive.

Forgive me when I downplay my own joy.
I don't mean to.
That's just my fear talking.
That's just old wounds whispering warnings.
That's just my knee-jerk response from a heart still healing.

I say things like,
"I know it won't always be like this",
and you shrink into yourself.
Your smile wilts like a dying rose that was full a moment ago.
My pain swallows the sun,
and I tell you I hate myself for projecting.
Your kindness refuses to allow me to speak to myself that way,
and I fall all over again.
And again.
And again.
And I swear to you,
I would go through another decade of wrought, hell, torment,
 and heartbreak,
if I knew you were the reward waiting.
You're my gift for not giving up,
when giving up was the only thing that made sense.
This is the greatest version I've ever been,
and I'm still accepting myself, it seems.
I'm not sure how you did it,
but you laid your hands on all my broken parts
and showed me
they never actually were.

My Shoulders

More important than giving you
everything I never had,
is instilling within you
everything I'm still trying to be.

I hope you always remember to treat yourself
with the kindness and compassion you deserve.
The kindness and compassion,
I know,
I sometimes withhold from myself.

I hope when you look in the mirror
you see yourself in every way I see you —
beautiful,
stunning inside and out.

I hope you never forget the way the world within you
can shape the one around you,
and you use everything you already are
to create one you're proud of.

I hope my shoulders always feel like home.
Whether to cry on,
or stand atop,
they are as strong as they are soft.

If love brings out the best in a person,
well, then
yours made me
the greatest version I'll ever be.

Forgive me,
because the example I'm trying to be
doesn't always come naturally.

There are broken parts of me
that only loving you could heal.

For every single lesson
learned on my own
there are a dozen others
only you could've shown.

Hurried

Please be careful with me.
I only act like I'm something indestructible.
When you've experienced the type of trauma I have,
you learn how to grieve quickly.
There was never much time to break.
The world never slowed down
for my suffering.
I was too young to understand how to heal.
My arms weren't strong enough
to hold myself together.
It was impossible to know which pieces
were meant to come with me
and which ones were meant to be left behind.

So, I carried the heaviest ones I could.

People believe me to be insensitive,
but they're wrong – I feel everything.
Too many wrong things, usually.
But I'm learning -
   to let my successes overshadow my mistakes,
that the love in my life
has always outweighed all the loss,
who to turn away from,
who it's safe to turn towards,
and that even though I've carried the heaviest pieces with me
all this time,
many of them were never actually mine.

Please be careful with me.
You're getting a side of me I rarely ever show.
A side I'm only now getting to know.

Until Then...

The time between now and feeling your body against mine
drags on painfully.
So slowly it's torturous.
I waste days fantasizing every way
you'll respond to my touch.
My mouth waters at the idea of us.
You tease me with every sly smile.
Every glance makes me shift in my seat.
You lick your lips, and I melt.
Everything about you is arousing.
And I realize then
that you know exactly what you're doing.
You're toying with me.
  Instigating me.
    Baiting me.
And it's working.

What I'm feeling goes far beyond lust.
This is carnal.
Something animalistic. Feral.
Nobody has ever desired you more than I do,
I promise you. I'm going to take my time.
I want the taste of you on my tongue.
Our fingers locked and pulling you in by your shoulders closer,
deeper into me.
This bed won't contain us.
Throw the sheets off.
Beg for more. Arch your back.
I want us on the floor.
I know you need this as much as I do.
I know the tension was rising in you just the same.
I'm going to learn your every curve
and the places that don't get touched often enough.
Let's drown in each other.
I want to watch you come down like rain.
Completely full,
until completely emptied.
I'll tell you when. I'll let you know when it's time.

Until then....

Everything Already

I don't need someone flawless.
I need someone frictionless.
Don't come to me with ideas.
Bring me your vision.
Show me that it's not hard to love someone still learning.
I don't need someone without problems.
I need someone who knows they're the answer.
I don't mind your obstacles,
so long as it's you and me
walking these roads together.
I don't need security. I need loyalty.
I don't need someone to bring me the world.
I need someone to show me that it's not so hurtful.
And that beautiful things can also be memorable.
I need someone to be everything I write home about.
I don't need someone to sit across from
or keep the other side of the bed warm.

I need someone to create a universe alongside.

My heart closes one door, and you open another.
By your side is the only place I've ever felt I belong.

I don't need your reassurance.
I need your resilience.
These mountains won't move themselves.
I don't need easy.
But can't we be each other's peace?
The storms don't stop.
Let's build a better shelter.
I don't need excuses.
I need us to be reason enough.
Really,
I don't need you to be anything more
than the everything you are
already.

Reads Like Graffiti

Honestly, I feel like I'm just beginning.
Like everything I've gone through in life
has been leading me to this moment.
Some of who I am,
   became who I was.
A necessary shedding of old layers outgrown.

I healed wounds I thought I never could.
I evolved into a person some thought I never would.
The reward wasn't retribution or revenge.
This version of me I became
was only made possible because of who broke me.
I'm proud of my pieces.
Grateful for the way they're fashioned together.

My life reads like graffiti.
Street art that's beautiful
   because it's gritty.
My views are kaleidoscopic.
I'm not sure where all this love and fire came from.
If it was there all along,
suppressed inside of me.
Or if they were little pieces collected along the way,
growing as I grew.
But this all feels fresh, brand new.
Like I'm on the cusp of something phenomenal.
Standing on the edge of brilliance.
Sometimes I forget how far I've come.
I'm in awe of my heart.
It's been through hell and still burns wildly.
From someone feeble and uninspired,
to someone enlivened and daring.
If you can't stand the way I shine now,
I suggest you stop staring.

Iridescent Skies

The only thing that's ever made sense to me is art.
The filthy, lonesome, bleeding arts.

Everything is romancing -
Train stations and railroad tracks.
Two-thirty in the morning,
and an out of tune guitar.
The crack and pop of a vinyl record,
and the crack and pop of a campfire.
A mother's love,
and a lover scorned,
fields of sunflowers,
and thunderstorms.
I obsess over the split second
before a first kiss
and sympathize with the drug addicts' last chance.
Old diners, burnt coffee,
and the little boy who just learned to ride a bike.
Home is wherever our favorite memories take shape.
And bliss is the stale smell
of a used bookstore.
Rain on a tin roof, a celestial serenade.
The single mother begging for overtime,
and an inmate saved by Jesus.
The feeling of feet stepping off the ledge,
and back on solid ground.
People who cry at concerts,
and renewing wedding vows.

There's a story in every gust of wind.
A poem born with each wave lapping the shore.
Life is far too extraordinary for me to ever live it ordinarily,
to not be awed.
The world is provocative.
So, I let it seduce me.
Rip my heart out,
and I'll make music with it.
We don't read and write poetry,
we live it.

Peaceful Trees

Shouldn't we be hurting one another by now?
Shouldn't we be cutting one another down by now?
I keep bracing for impact,
and you keep showing me that love isn't something to be afraid of.
All the love I've ever known was septic.
Something violent and reckless.
Give me some time to trust the softness of your edges.
Stay in my way.
Let me breathe you in.
Let me share your air.

We spend our days finding ourselves
in one another.
Sitting beneath peaceful trees.
The grass is so green here.
You tell me I deserve to feel this good.
And for the first time,
I believe that may be true.
You did more than just make room within your world.
You shared the most beautiful parts of it.
Then made space in mine
for beautiful things of my own to grow.
Things others felt I was beneath
you brought to life naturally.

I can't help but notice little synchronicities now.
You tell me they mean I'm right where I'm meant to be.
And for the first time, I feel seen.
Understood. Accepted. Received. Free.

All my life I've been searching for more
yet settling for less.
Accepted a purpose for myself far smaller than the one I have now.
I'm not sure I ever actually understood love
until you showed me I'm someone worth loving.

Make Me A Fool

You made a fool of me.
In all the greatest ways.

What's funny is how we were both so certain we weren't ready.
We were too broken to bend.
Too raw to be felt.
And because fast is the only way we know how to fall,
we knew better than to jump at all.

When you heal and reassemble yourself,
giving your heart away is no longer something you do carelessly.
You're not as brave as you believed.
But you can't hide from what's meant for you.
You can't outrun future and fate.

I'm afraid.
Every part of me is terrified. That's the truth.
I tell myself to move slowly, carefully,
knowing damn well that the love inside me is always overwhelming.
Engulfing and potent.
Something intimidating to the timid.
And because I don't know how to love with half of my heart,
I figured it was best not to love at all.
It was safer in the shadows.
Then you brought me light.
You took something wild, out of control,
and calmed it.
When I attempted to quell the fires growing inside of me,
you reached for my hand
and danced in the flames.

They lied when they said, "you're never ready".
I might not have been looking for what we share
but I see now that everything I survived,
every painful lesson learned,
was in preparation for this moment.
I've never been more ready
for the love I deserve.

Equal Energy

The reality is,
you've never been given a chance to be soft.
To relax.
To relinquish.
From the very beginning,
you were forced into a role that demanded
you be in control.
And though you flourish as a leader,
you desire something other than sovereignty.

You've always been the one who was relied upon,
yet rarely had anyone to rely on.

And oh, how sweet it would be to just float.
To just drift and flow and feel the freedom
of getting lost in someone you trust.
To sink into the embracing arms of someone unwavering.
Someone so fiercely loyal
that when you look in their eyes
you see an unbreakable bond.
You deserve an energy equal to your own.
Someone whose ambition and drive rises to meet you
exactly where you are.
Where you've always been.

For so long you've carried the weight of unmet promises
that turned into burdens.
This is not your fault.
Look how far you've come.
It's easier to walk these roads alone
than it is to drag someone along.
All you ever ask for in return
are the very same things you give away freely.
Stop excusing your expectations.
You deserve reciprocation.

I Choose You

This is important - you and I are meant to be,
and that, alone,
is not enough.
We must be great.
We must tend to our garden daily.

Love is an action. A verb.
An expression that transcends words.
Love forever honors effort
and rewards the work.
Love lives in the everyday details.
Woven within small acknowledgments and selfless gestures.
Kindness and compassion must be customary.
Forgiveness is never the exception.
And let us never forget that intimacy grows
from energy and affection,
not time.
We must be deliberate.
We must be strong.
We must make steel from iron hearts
and be forged from every fiery adversity.

Let's breathe life into our blessings
and make joy the priority.
Finding one another was merely the beginning.
Forever is only this moment.
Fate becomes what we make true.
Every day there's a decision.
And every day, in every way,
I choose you.

Learning To Love

The hardest work I've ever done was internal.
Identifying and repairing parts of myself
painful to the touch.
Reconstructing all the rooms
housing my heart.
I like my anguish locked away.
Hidden, as to not make others uncomfortable.

I believed I needed to be different.
Called myself *introverted* when fear kept me isolated.
Mercurial was synonymous with *anxious*.
Rather than heal my wounds,
I learned how spin them into something you might think
made me unique.
I'm still learning to love the child inside me
who grew up too soon.

I want the six-year-old me to know those prayers will be answered,
but in ways you won't understand until later.
Please, do not be afraid. It's going to be ok. Rest. Sleep now.

I want the eight-year-old me to know they are deserving of love.
It is coming.
But it will not come from the ones you most need it from.
Be patient. This isn't your fault.
This will not be your home for long.

I want to tell the ten-year-old me to be brave –
this year will be the worst.
It'll teach you how to hurt in ways you will remember forever.
But you will survive.
It's ok to be afraid. It's ok to cry. Protect your brother. He's afraid, too.
Be for him, who you needed for yourself.

I think I've spent too much time worried about who I became,
and not nearly enough time
with the child inside me still in need of conscling.
A past unrepaired
keeps the future unsecured.

J. Raymond

I'm Learning

Being alone requires bravery.
Only in solitude do you discover parts of yourself
you might not be proud of.

How can I expect the love I'm deserving of
while I'm unwilling to even show myself enough?
Pain becomes familiar.
Unrelenting grief is the worst,
most reliable companion.

But solitude also unearths inner strength.
I learned how to grow quietly.
For myself, for once.
And heartache
   that was once a headwind,
became the breeze at my back.
Moving me forward and further away
from familiar pains
each day.

It's not easy to give yourself credit
when you've always accepted the blame.

Believe me though,
   I'm learning.

It won't be long now before the rest of the world sees on the outside,
all the changes that took place in the dark.
I know well the work required
for the life I desire.
And since I've gone through hell already,
that doesn't intimidate me.
When you've spent much of your life either struggling, suffering, or healing,
dreaming doesn't come naturally.
And still, I shed the dead weight and dream.

I found joy and success even while carrying a heavy heart.
But this newfound lightness excites me.

Yes, I Am

I like rare things.
Challenging, complex things.
The untouched, elusive,
and hard to hold onto.
Mysterious things that are often misunderstood
and overlooked.

I like things I see some of myself within.
I can't help but value what others underestimate.
I root for the underdog,
because I am the underdog.
I shouldn't be here,
and there's pride in the fact that I am.
I defy logic.
I oppose the odds.
I believe in magic,
and see it in places many others don't think to look.

Popular beliefs and common knowledge aren't exciting.
I like contrarian things.
Unusual and peculiar things.
I like outliers and anomalies.
If everyone has had it, I don't want it.
If everyone has touched it, and loved it,
I know it's not meant for me.
Because I, myself,
am not easy to touch or love.

Abstract things have hidden beauty.
I appreciate those things in you,
because I've learned to appreciate those things in me.

To Be Known

What I really crave now is intimacy.
Everything else feels shallow in comparison.
My soul wants to be recognized.
To be known intrinsically.

I don't need another warm body
or tepid, fleeting company.
I need someone transcendent.
Someone inspired and intoxicating.

This is why I fall fast -
I'm more afraid of wasting time
than I am of being hurt.

Intimacy grows slowly, deliberately.
But connection happens quickly, uncontrollably.
Attraction is merely a fire starter.
Lust, a matchbox.
But it's intimacy which keeps embers aglow.
Growing hotter over time.
I want someone to evolve with.
To feel from the inside-out.
We are mountains,
not steppingstones.
We are bodies of water that run deep.
We are undiscovered galaxies,
and I crave adventure.
Is it possible for someone to value my life,
just as much as their own?

I don't want someone to grow old with.
I want someone to stay young alongside.

Show Me

They don't talk much about how difficult
a healthy relationship can be for those still healing.
Peace feels confusing
when most of the love you've known
is volatile and toxic.

You bring flowers,
but we see a scythe.
Kind words land like linen white lies.
It's unnatural to accept acceptance -
that someone could love you without motives,
or that we won't soon be hung by the strings
we weren't even aware were attached.
And that maybe we truly can be loved
for exactly who we are
and given a chance to outgrow our flaws.

I'm tired of apologizing for the way I fall.
A part of me awaits and expects the floor to drop out
from beneath my feet.
And that one day I'll wake up and realize
the beauty around me was all a dream.
That's not your fault.
I'm trying to unlearn what I've been taught love means.
My heart has carried more blame than credit.

When you say I'm perfect for you,
I don't see what you see.
Please, show me.
My stories haven't had happy endings,
so it's hard to believe that this time
it'll be different.
I want to believe.
Despite everything I've been shown,
I still hold onto hope that everything I am
might be everything you want
and need.

Earn The Person

At the very least, be honest with her.
She expects effort,
not perfection.
Nobody is unscathed at this point in life.
None of us are entirely intact.

There's no sense pretending to be someone you aren't.
Attempting to appease her today,
only to disappoint her tomorrow,
is senseless.
Don't waste her time.
Don't allow her to invest in something flimsy and fraudulent.

Allow her to decide for herself
if you're somebody she could grow alongside.
Our hearts are on the line here.
Be brave enough to admit your shortcomings,
then resolve to improve upon them.
Make weighty promises you intend to keep.
Be unwavering and fiercely consistent.
Respect the fact that she's been hurt
on profoundly deep levels,
and swear to handle her compassionately.
If you know,
in your heart,
that you can't do those things,
don't even open the door to hers.
Don't begin building something atop a foundation
that's already compromised.
Leave her to her dreams.
Don't stand in the way of her own peace and happiness,
just because you want to feel her warmth across your skin.
Don't block her sunlight
simply because you like the way she shines.

If you're not ready to be what she deserves,
admitting it is admirable.
That's life.
We're all growing at different speeds....

Sometimes, the best thing you can do for a woman
who's come as far as she has
is just leave her be.
Be *exactly* who you are.
Your true self.
So that the destiny intended for you finds its way.

One of the greatest things you can do for your life
is work on yourself
until you earn the person meant for you.

My Universe

Give me lazy love.
I used to fantasize over grand gestures
and wild adventures.
But the vast majority of our days together
will be far simpler.
Not spent sky diving and jet-setting.
There's nothing I enjoy more than slow, dawdling days
spent in bed together, laughing, eating,
making love in between episodes of some show we're hardly watching.

You're my universe.
Stunning without trying.
You nestle further, sink deeper into me,
as if you can't get close enough.
But I feel you in my bones.
In my soul already.
I feel your smile against my chest,
and another little piece of me is made whole.

I love knowing that you know
how safe you are with me.
That's not something either of us has had much of in the past.
We breathe each other in,
and our spirits exhale – finally, we're at peace.
Doing nothing whatsoever with you
is my favorite thing to do.
You make the mundane feel magical.
Whatever extravagant dreams I once had for myself
have been replaced by ones where you're at the center of.
A warm home filled with music, dancing, and all the things we love.
I crave time together, making you smile,
you should know just how much you are appreciated.
I no longer need the grandiose
because with the right person,
your person,
all you need is their company for life to feel adventurous.

We make fire from just the energy between us
and the little corner of the world we share
fills with purpose.

Running Starts

I don't dabble.
All in, or all out.
People like me might tend to put things off,
though it isn't as simple as procrastination.

We just can't seem to take on anything casually.
We pour ourselves into passions.

I don't investigate first.
I fully immerse.
I don't peek around corners.
I jump off cliffs from running starts.
There's nothing neutral, muted, or tepid
about me.
Maybe it's the addictive personality,
but I crave oceans and feeling overwhelmed.
My thirst is rarely quenched.
My fires never quelled.
My heart either beats wildly for the thing,
or ignores it completely.

If I seem slow to move at times,
it's only because I'm not yet certain if what's in front of me
deserves my devotion.
Art, music, people, experiences,
even the simplest tasks are all-consuming.
But listen, my obsessive compulsions also mean
I take my commitments more seriously than others seem to.
If I care about you, you will know.
It'll be obvious.
My promises are binding.
If you're a part of my world,
you'll know loyalty.
So please understand what you're asking for when asking for me.
Giving myself away is costly,
and I won't be the same person
once on the other side us.

Warrier Sisters

You and I are proof that friends can be soulmates, too.
We share a rare bond.
A connection beyond uncommon.
The same scar across my heart
  adorns yours.
Those pains didn't simply make us stronger,
they brought us closer together.
Making us sisters.
Turning us into warriors.

But you should know,
I'm in awe of you – your strength.
To witness your resilience,
and see up close
your perseverance
is inspiring.
You climbed the mountain until you became one.
Now, we all look up to you.
The simple act of knowing you
makes us better.
But to call you a friend
is an honor.
You turned your life into an adventure
that those closest are lucky to experience.
I consider myself the luckiest of them all.
Look how far we've come.
And the way our roads converged.
Look what we made of the hardships and heartbreaks.
We are unconditional.
Everlasting, with no strings attached, accepted entirely as we are.
And though there's still so much to look forward to, please know that
your story will always be my favorite story.

For as long as you are here,
know that you are loved.
And forever,
  after that.

Closer To

With the wrong one it's never enough.
Moments of bliss are short lived.
You bleed and bleed and bleed,
and it never matters more than how they feel.
You exhaust yourself attempting to create a world to their liking.
Catering to their every whim.
And all you get in return is disproval.

But with the right one,
each one of your rough edges
seem like eccentricities.
With the right one, you can't lose.
It's all a lesson.
An opportunity to create more unity.
Forging one another through fires.
Obstacles are only things to grow over,
not roadblocks you're walled behind.

I'm convinced that the greatest thing we can offer one another
is acceptance.
How many of us have wasted years
convinced we weren't enough?
With the right one, you won't need to ask.
You won't need to beg.
You won't scream to be heard.
You won't bleed to be seen.
With the right one
pain isn't commonplace
and perfection isn't expected.

Everything you're becoming takes you further
from the ones who won't appreciate it,
and closer to the ones awaiting it.

In The Meantime

I believe we're just one person away
from being loved in all the greatest ways.
One person away
from understanding how necessary and perfect
our path was
all along.
One chance encounter away
from every misstep making sense.
Every heartbreak being mended.
Every wound being soothed.

We try our best to be that for ourselves,
but the truth is
not everything broken inside of us is our doing.
Some of the damage dealt
came at the hands of someone else.

It took time for me to trust a gentle touch.
Allowing someone to fall for me
became more challenging
than falling myself.
Because I knew my intentions.
I understood my own motives.
It was others I was unsure of.
Turns out that every person I've ever given myself to
was absolutely essential to my growth.
Towards me arriving where I am today.
Every disappointment was a prerequisite.
The ones who hurt me, taught me how to heal.
The ones who left me,
gifted me independence.
Some brought peace.
Others brought pain.
And every single one of them helped me learn who I am,
and,
who I refuse to be.
There are spaces within me that can only be filled
by love I cannot show myself.
I know that now.
But just because they're empty at times,

doesn't mean the rest of me isn't overflowing.
I don't notice a void, or something missing.
I only see opportunity,
more possibility.

I'll continue giving myself everything I can
in the meantime.

The Beauty I See

I'm at a point in life where I'm content in the present.
I don't fantasize over the future.
I'm not hung up on what could've been,
what should've been,
who hurt me,
what I'm owed,
what's fair, unfair, right, wrong,
or any single thing I can't go back and do differently.
I'm not who I was.
I'm moving deliberately, with love.
Protecting and padding my peace.
Forgiving quickly.
Setting boundaries.
Expressing gratitude freely.

I'm closer to the person I envisioned than ever before.
I learned my lessons, and grew from places
I still can't make sense of.

I'm not reliving long nights,
singing sad songs,
and commiserating over campfires that feel like purgatories.
I'm not pretending to be someone I'll never be.
The best of me
is someone to be proud of, already.
I'm not begrudged, burdened,
or looking over my shoulder.
I'm not daydreaming.
I'm not waiting.
I'm not begging.
I'm not pleading.
I'm not wishing.
I'm not forcing anything in or out

of my life.
I'm listening.
I'm receiving.
I'm wide open.

The inside of my head and heart was once hellish.
A neglected and abused place.
But not anymore.
It's flourishing.
Plush and succulent.
Somewhere teeming with appreciation.
Nothing toxic can survive here.
Nothing limiting or critical thrives here.

I'd give you my eyes and show you were to look,
but the beauty I see
exists within me.

I Meant To Tell You

The last time we spoke I meant to tell you -
I think you're incredible.
But the words got stuck in my throat.
You should know that I think of you all the time.
You deserve to hear it said aloud,
so I'm sorry for not saying what's spilling out of my heart.

Everything I do these days is with you in mind.
I'll walk by a beautiful home
and imagine us inside one of our own.
I hold off on trying new restaurants
because I know I'll enjoy them more with you.
Postcards become places I envision us vacationing.
I leave myself notes of questions to ask you,
or things I found funny
that I know you will, too.
You're the best, most beautiful part of my life.
Woven into the fabric of my days.

Sometimes,
I talk myself out of telling you how wildly proud of you I am.
Kind words weren't something I heard often growing up.
They still feel awkward and clumsy leaving my lips.
It's easier for me to write them down.
So,
I hope these words land just the same.
I hope you're reading this in my voice and hear it how I do –
I'm so proud of you, sweetheart.
Life grows so hectic at times,
and I'm sure you feel as if you're spinning your wheels,
wondering when it'll get easier,
or if all your hard work is worth it.
I see the way you push yourself
and how life sometimes pushes back.
I see the way exhaustion shows up too early on long days.
You glance in the mirror and joke about how tired you look.
But you should know that all I see
is your strength.
Your eyes look like home to me.
All I see is the rest of my life.
If you ever,

for even one second,
feel as if you're not doing enough,
please know that couldn't be further from the truth.

I'm sorry I didn't say this earlier,
when we spoke,
but you are incredible.
I'm here,
whenever you need somewhere to rest.
I'll remind you again then.

Long Enough

One of the greatest gifts my past has given me
is a crystal-clear understanding of the future I deserve.

If this is my last day here,
I plan on dancing across the threshold.
I will spend it lovingly,
making a few more beautiful memories
to leave behind.
I will not waste these final breaths
berating myself.

Truthfully, if I could go back and do anything differently,
I would have shown myself the love I knew I needed.
I waited too long for flowers that never arrived.
I should've sewn seeds
and made my own Spring sumptuous.
Grown my own luxuriant world.
I would have lived my life a bit more selfishly,
pursued my own passions more courageously.

However,
I refuse to view my own generosity as a shortcoming.
My heart is not a martyr.
Kindness will not be my regret.
Though much of my life has been spent going uphill,
it made me appreciate the views that much more.
Those closest to me
became some of the most painful parts of the journey,
so, forgive me if I choose to walk alone for a moment.
I don't mind the quiet.
My solitude is serene.
There's more road behind me than ahead,
and I intend to make every step remaining
as beautiful and peaceful as possible.
I'm growing lighter the further I go.
Releasing remorse.
Embracing relief.
I've carried burdens long enough.
What's left of me will get the best of me.

Rosewood

I like how you're powerful and don't even know it.
Your modesty makes you look away whenever complimented.
But it's true.
I only say it because I see it
in the way you cling to dreams.
Dreams you could've easily given up on.
Yet you haven't quit.
You're not settling or going through the motions
and counting down your days.
You still want the world for yourself
and those you share it with.

I say that you're powerful
because I know the list of letdowns is long.
Your heart's been broken in ways few would believe.
Now you keep the stories to yourself.
You've learned to sing sad songs quietly.
You bleed privately.
I know how difficult it is to be cut down
while trying to move through life lovingly.
It's a choice you made long ago,
and continue to make daily.
To hope. To show up. To stay true.
You view the world through
rose-colored glasses of every hue.
Every shade.
Every shadow.

I like how powerful you are
even when you believe yourself weak.
Even when worried.
How many times have you started over?
And still.... here you stand.
Powerful in ways you've yet to grasp.
Powerful, not because you've never lost or been beaten.
But because you have
and are better for it.

J. Raymond

On Your Skin

I am the full moon. I am the howl.
I am transformative.
I am a tectonic shift.

Do not come to me seeking refuge.
I am not a shoulder in need
of someone's tears.
I am a storm the spiritless should fear.
I am a multitude. I am overwhelming.
I am turned all the way on.
All the way up.
I am not ashamed, ordinary, or replaceable.
I am the hooks sunk deep
you don't want removed.
I am visceral and primal.
I am something like lightning.
The one you can't shake.
The one who gets away.
The one wide awake, unafraid,
and no longer waiting.
I am a midnight masquerade
you can't keep your hands off.
I am who you pull in close on cold nights.
I am who you kiss in dark alleys
and get lost in the city alongside.
I am the irresistible scent on your skin,
the taste you crave on your lips,
the one you will never forget.
I turn boring worlds upside down,
and paint sunrises across night skies.
I am the one you never saw coming.
I am love and lust and warmth and water
all rolled into one.
I am fireworks. I am explosive.
I am not for the faint of heart.
I am music. I am passion.
I don't make art.
I am art.

Chance To Grow

Maybe what I'm most proud of is that,
despite every letdown and disappointment,
I chose to continue wholeheartedly believing
in love.

And though my world has been rocked before,
I never once imagined it devoid.
I fought to remain a place where beautiful things
had a chance to grow.

Do you know how amazing it is
to see someone bloom in front of you?
To watch them shake free from their fears
and insecurities
and finally break through.

Maybe it isn't that she's jaded
as much as she's afraid.
People bring hells into homes
and leave us in ruins.
Maybe all she needs is someone safe
to be herself alongside.

It seems so simple,
but the world will strip you of your authenticity.
People will convince you that your individuality isn't enough.
We learn early how to hide ourselves from even those
we're supposed to trust.
We keep love and affection out of arms reach,
just far enough away
that it won't cut us too deep.
Be her sanctuary.
Be somewhere she can feel out loud
and stretch her arms out wide
and just be whoever the hell she's been the entire time.
Watch an extraordinary world pour out of her
and brighten everything it touches.

Warmth To Winter

I truly thought something was wrong with me before I met you.

A few who didn't mind twisting knives told me,
  "Nobody will ever love you like I do",
until I soon believed it was romantic to bleed.
Pain was the price you paid for passion.
Every time I fell for another's promise and touch,
it took a little more to piece myself back together.
You can only break in new ways so many times
before you just stop trying.
Before you learn the only person who can be trusted is yourself –
and even that isn't always so.

It's hard to believe that everything was a lesson
in how to love myself better,
for you.
I was becoming strong enough for us both.
Someone enough for us both.

Now, I can't help but turn you into a poem.
The way I hear songbirds in your laughter,
and how you're the only thing I've ever been addicted to
that gives me life.
You bring me sunlight.
You sow benevolence in places that've only housed hate.
You don't know this but,
each time you reach for my hand, I swear
my entire soul stretches in your direction.
You bring warmth to winter seasons.
My life always had meaning,
only, now it has reasons.
I will not fail you. I will not fail us.

When I think of those times I was told
  "nobody will ever love you like I do",
I can't help but smile and think to myself,
"that's what I'm hoping for".

Touch The Sun

Nothing drains me like negativity.
I crave people who help me find my way back to myself.
One thing you should know about me –
   I'm following my heart from here on out.

I've seen the way it makes mosaics
of broken things.
Stop bringing me your skepticisms
and doubts
and telling me all the reasons why my dreams should stay small.
This world is littered with scrutiny.
Crumpled up fears thrown at the backs
of those going somewhere
most others are too afraid to venture.
If you can't fan my flames,
don't you dare douse them.
When I show you the flowers inside of me,
don't pull them because all you know
are weeds.
They took a lifetime to grow.
   Let my cup overflow.
      Let me touch the sun.
Bring wind to my sails, not rain.

I've already considered everything concerning.
Obsessed over it.
Picked it apart.
So, if you see me madly in love,
or running wild after something you can't comprehend,
just know that it was never meant for you to.

Less Than Hunger

The person I'm trying most to make proud is myself.
It's not so simple.
I know too much. I feel too much.
I'm so much sometimes
that I'm not even sure where to begin.
My therapist tells me I need to heal my "inner child".
And I wonder how many others also struggle
to wrap their arms around a version of themselves
who grew up too soon.
I open my mouth, and all my fears fall out.
I meant to say *"I love you"*
but all that spills out is
"you're not enough".

My pride needs reassurance,
and I thought I'd have outgrown that by now.
I thought the version of me who survived
would be more confident.
Maybe once I'm proud of myself,
others will be, too?
Maybe once I can see in myself some of the good I see in all of you,
I'll start feeling it, too?
I'll stand in front of the mirror
and see more answers than questions.
More success than failure.
More friend than foe.

It's almost as if the younger version of me accepted early
that they were undeserving.
If you don't want what your heart is starved for,
it hurts less than hunger itself.
You stop asking for love
and begin feeding yourself reasons why it isn't meant for you.

The person I'm trying most to make proud is myself.
I open up my heart, and all my love falls out.
I meant to keep a little for myself,
but you looked like you could use some.

And I guess that's something to be proud of.

You Still Deserve

You still deserve to be loved
in all the ways you want.
You still deserve to be embraced,
you still deserve to be valued,
you still deserve to be seen as someone significant.

It doesn't matter if you've had it before and lost it,
or you've never felt love's fiery touch.
It doesn't matter how far off path you've gone to arrive in this place.
It doesn't matter how wrong you've been,
how much anguish or deceit you've experienced.
So long as there's a heart beating brazenly
in your chest,
so long as your lungs run chasing
after its breath,
you deserve a love which sets you free.
You deserve to be awed.
You deserve someone who wants to read every word of your story.
You deserve someone who can't take their eyes off the way you shine.
You deserve someone who admires what it took for you to arrive here,
and respects the rough roads traveled on your way to them.
You deserve someone who isn't above showing compassion and affection.
You still deserve someone who knows you've been strong for so long
and gives you space to be weak.
You still deserve someone who sees everything beneath the surface,
beyond the flaws, into everything you are.

I know that going through hell strips us of dreams,
but you still deserve all the things you stopped wishing for.

Smoke In Your Eyes

I'm too exhausted to be outraged.
Not even sure where to direct my incense,
so I just let it rise.
Careful not to get smoke in your eyes.
It's ironic how each generation thinks the one following theirs
has it easier,
yet we can all agree things only seem to be getting worse.
We hate one another so much
that we can hardly even agree on facts.
We fund wars with money that's endlessly taxed,
and even our food is trying to kill us.
EV batteries are the new blood diamonds.
Our children are bought and sold like produce
and hardly anyone looks up from their phone long enough to notice.
Half pull one way.
Half pull the other.
Now we're stretched so thin our American dreams are anemic.

We glorify people so far removed from our own world
we might as well be worshipping aliens.
Consume.
Scroll.
Work.
Escape.
Argue.
Sleep.
Eat.
Offend.
Protest.
Do nothing.
Act interested.
Pretend to know.
Pretend to take a stand.
Make no difference.
Blame the wrong people.
Vote.
Fight amongst ourselves,

about issues out of our control.
Buy another gun.
Abort the baby too late.
Pray. Riot. Cry.
Watch T.V. Watch the news. Watch the video.
Watch this.
Watch that.
Just watch.
Stay distracted.
Stay woke.
Tell me what to fight for.
Tell me what to die for.
Tell me why I'm wrong.
Tell me why you're right.
Quick, find someone to disagree with.
Quick, find something to hate.
Spit vitriol and venom.
Show 'em how far you can urinate.
Bled blue. Bled red. Bled for a cause.
Bled out.
Don't complain too much
or they'll give you something to cry about.

I'd show you where the beauty is hidden,
but not enough are interested enough
for it to make any difference.

Without You

This is not where I imagined myself.
This is not the life I had planned.
The world I poured myself into did not look like the one
in which I'm now standing.
It took time – to get upright,
to breathe,
to heal.
And when you're in the middle of breaking
it becomes quite clear that you will never be the same after this.
These pieces will never fit back together
as they once were.
How foolish I was for believing I was safe.
For placing my heart,
my life,
my future in the hands of someone
reaching for another.

It was easier for you to convince yourself
that I was somehow the enemy,
than accept your own indiscretions.

All these years later, and you still reach for me
when you're struggling,
when you're hurting,
when you're feeling all the things I once felt.
Somedays I feel the sun across my skin
and just smile at how far I've come.
Anger and sadness long subsided.
You made me prioritize myself.

Destroying the world I knew,
allowed me to create the one I deserve,
without you.
I'm grateful for the devastation
in ways that only grow more beautiful
over time.

How Could I?

The person I am now
is so loyal to the one I'm becoming
that being alone is better than settling.

This is what trusting yourself looks like.
This is what hard-earned faith looks like.
You see, it's not that I believe my path will be easy.
It's that I'm so sure of my strength
I no longer stress it.
I accept what is.
I accept what isn't.
I welcome every lesson with open arms, heart, and mind.

This is what making it through to the other side looks like.
This is what fortitude and nerve looks like.
It's not you and I against the world.
It's you and I aligned with it,
so that you and I exist within it.

The universe isn't conspiring against us.
It's bending in our favor. Stop resisting.
How could I not think the world of myself
when stitched this way?
How could I hate myself
knowing everything I've already overcome?
How could I dread the road ahead
when the worst is already behind me?

I wasted so many years breaking my own heart
over things needing to be set free.
I sunk claws and teeth into people and dreams
that were only ever intended to be lessons.

I want you with me,
but if you come into my world with the wrong energy,
me leaving
will be the lesson you receive.

You Brought Hope Back

I don't think you understand just how much you mean to me.
I'm still making sense of it myself.
There wasn't much hope left in me
by the time you arrived
Sacrificing myself for another
wasn't a risk I was willing to take.

I was content building a softer world.
One without sharp edges.
I'd exhausted myself painting skies
in everyone else's favorite colors
until I had no clue what views I might like.
Every person I'd ever loved
turned into a tragedy.
Someone I couldn't hold properly,
or who had no idea what to make of me.
You were the first person who made
being struck by lightning
feel safe.
You brought home pieces of me I didn't realize were missing.
Gave me sustenance.
Loving you almost feels involuntary, magnetic.
It's as if the universe was merely waiting for me to love myself correctly
before sending someone capable of doing the same.
You brought hope back to a hopeless romantic
and helped me paint kaleidoscopic skies of my own.

Is destiny what's happening
while we're foolishly making plans?

You're proof that I'm deserving of more than I've been shown before,
and that nothing is an accident.
Maybe we weren't two souls who met,
as much as we were two souls finally ready
to reconnect.

Too Much

You're right – I am too much.
I've got too much to offer to see myself through your eyes.
I've got too much going for me to waste time wondering
why you thought I was someone worth wrecking.

I've got too much pride to stomach lies from anyone puerile.
I've got too much fire pent up to spend on lukewarm lovers.

I am too much.
I'm too much of all the things that make me
problematic for anyone believing I'm one to take advantage of.
I'm too intuitive to be gaslit.
I'm too steady to stand beside your wavering.
I'm too loyal to overlook your insincerity.
I've worked too hard,
come too far,
to be convinced that the very best parts of me
need to be quelled or toned down,
simply because it's intimidating to you.

I should intimidate you.
I should move you.
I'm supposed to awaken parts within which scare you a bit.
I bet it's frustrating
how I just won't mindlessly acquiesce.
I bet it's impossible for you to understand that,
perhaps,
you aren't enough.

Either way, you're right – for you,
I am too much.

It's About Time

It's about time I say goodbye.
To anyone and anything
no longer bringing out the best in me.
To memories too painful to continue carrying.
To behaviors and habits
that don't propel me onward, upward,
and in the direction of my dreams.

It's about time I say goodbye to what I thought my life
was supposed to look like
and get busy creating the one meant for me.
It's about time I grieve and give myself
the closure I've waited on long enough.

It's about time I say goodbye
to these old demons I no longer need as company.
It's about time I bury my burdens
and allow new possibilities to grow wildly.
It's about time I forgave those who hurt me instead of healing themselves.
It's about time I accept that
protecting myself is respecting myself.
It's about time I say goodbye to a few who were once blessings,
became a curse,
and now will serve merely as lessons.
It's about time I close the doors that led me this far
but will take me no further.

And it's about time I say hello to everything I've kept waiting,
and those on their own journey alongside me.
It's time to make new memories.
It's time I turn these dreams into reality.

And now, I'll say goodbye to who I was,
forever grateful for getting me this far.
Goodbye to the parts of myself that didn't survive,
and hello to the version of me only possible
because the best of me did.

Make Yourself Sick

I heard you were asking about me.

Which means your better options fell through.
Which means the grass must not have been greener.
Which means the sun set,
and you still can't stand yourself.

Don't tell me you miss me.
You seemed so sure when you left,
weren't worried about me at all —
don't pretend to care now.
I warned you my tears would dry
before you realized what you lost,
and you wouldn't listen.
You moved on so quickly,
like I was nothing, and now you're backpedaling.
Keep running.
I bet it's exhausting trying to fix the world around you
and never the one within you.
I bet you've got to swallow your lies just to sleep at night.
The irony is you used say I was playing the victim,
and now you're the one needing saving.
I'm not even surprised.
Go find another forever for a while.
Go fill every void with anyone unsuspecting,
while you still can.
Until you make yourself as sick as I am
for all that time I'll never get back.
Time you'll be stuck recounting
Memories you'll keep revisiting.
At least now you know what it feels like.

Honestly, it was great to hear from you.

Antibodies

Even when walking away
moved her in the right direction
quitting would never come easily.
Damaged things could be repaired.
Broken people could be mended.
Every day,
an opportunity for the tides to turn,
the chains to break,
and the words she deserves
to finally be heard.

The days are piling up behind her.
Growing mountains to stand atop,
not be buried beneath.

Some of what you're most reluctant to give up on
are the pieces needing to go missing.
Letting go doesn't make you weak.
Strength isn't your body growing tolerable
of poison it was never meant to take.
Quit the things killing you.
Pull deep, exhilarating breaths
into exhausted lungs.
Resuscitate yourself.
Run free from whatever holds you hostage.
There's no shame in changing seasons.

Where death walks, life follows.

Choose Your Rains

You don't see yourself the way I see you.

One day, when I tell you you're amazing,
the voice in your head
will only echo in agreement.
You aren't your shortcomings.
Those imperfections you believe to be glaring
are unnoticeable to me.
You aren't the flaws you try to hide.
You aren't the mistakes you've made.
You aren't the abuse you took.

Please understand that to me, you're heroic,
so it's difficult to hear you speak of yourself with resentment.
You undermine the bridges you rebuilt,
while I'm in awe of the world you grew from nothing.
You don't understand how much
you mean to me.
You don't realize how colorless my life would become
if you weren't in it.
Even when it's dark you shine on me.
I would choose your rain
over anyone else's sunlight.
I would choose your cold nights
over any warm body.
You are the realest thing I've ever loved,
and I don't want a single day without you.

I know it's hard to unlearn all the things this world has convinced you
are wrong about yourself.
So, I'll point out every star I see in you
until the night skies you carry are blinding.
I'll shower you with the words you never heard enough of
until that voice in your head believes what I know is true –
You are loved.
You are beautiful.
You are everything.

Not In Between, But Both

I'm a conundrum.
A mixed bag of emotions and desires.
I want wildness yet crave the serene.
I want colorful explosions,
and I want to stay in bed all day.
I want my mind warped in all the right ways,
yet I want to be sure of myself.

I want to run amuck,
make a complete mess of things,
and I also want to live a nice, tidy life.
I want to lay eyes on parts of the world
which baffle me,
but I also want a home so warm
I dread leaving it.
I want threadbare luggage
and a worn-out passport,
but I also want to drink coffee with the same group of friends
at the same time and place each day.
I want adventure, but I want consistency.
I want the unfamiliar, and to form a routine.
I long for opposite ends of the spectrum, polarities,
and feeling out of place.
But I also want to stop running for once,
and enjoy the heavens already around me.
There's a part of me that will always be a junkie,
in love with the adrenaline rush.
And there's a part of my heart that only wants to rest and beat slowly.

I found happiness once I stopped trying to live somewhere in between
and tearing myself in two.
I am both things - a proud anomaly
who gave wings to hypocrisies,
allowing even the misunderstood parts to be true.

In Stitches

Ever since I was young I've hidden my smile.
In nearly every photo,
a sly, sealed tight grin, holding in my insecurities.
My face would grow red and warm whenever someone would say
"Come on! Smile!".
So, I'd pin the corners of my mouth a little higher up my cheeks.

Showing the world my happiness felt forced.
When I couldn't contain my own laugh,
I'd set it free with my back turned to you.
Eventually I just stopped smiling altogether.
Soon people started saying that I always looked angry, unapproachable, scary.
I heard it so often
I believed I was all those things.
And that's how it went for years and years.
All my joy, all my most favorite memories,
stifled behind my crooked smile.

Until one day, a friend sent a photo of me taken unsuspectingly,
in which I'm laughing hysterically.
Completely in stitches.
Damn near to tears.
"You have a great smile! Love this pic of you", they said.

You see,
sometimes we hide the very best parts of ourselves
for no other reason than we're afraid they won't be received.
We deprive the world of our laughter,
our creativity,
our uniqueness,
because it's imperfect.
I'll never be impeccable,
and you'll never be flawless,
and maybe all we really need is someone to remind us
that it's safe to come outside.
That we have, in fact,
always been valuable.

Smile wide and I will, too.
Everybody loves it when we do.

The Best of Me

If you're lucky enough,
the universe will send you someone
who turns your entire world inside out.

I knew the instant I laid eyes on you
that you were the most important person in my life.
That hasn't changed.
It's only grown stronger and brighter over time.

Like lightning, love comes out of nowhere.
It reaches through you with hands so reassuring and familiar
you swear you've felt them in another lifetime.
You brought me pieces I forgot were missing.
Healed parts others mistreated and discarded.
Put a broken spirit back intact.
And I'm not sure I'll ever be able to do as much for you
as you've done for me.
But I'll try.
Please know that the only future I care about experiencing
is the one we're enjoying together.

You are beautiful and inspiring in ways
 you don't see.
Compassionate and selfless in ways
which never go unnoticed.
We're in the middle of our greatest adventure,
and you are the safest home I've ever known.
If there's a point to life,
you will always be at the heart of mine.
The very best of me
is you.

Flow Forward

Right now,
the only person you need to trust and forgive,
is yourself.

For most of your life you've had to fight
and earn every ounce of happiness.
You've pushed and pulled.
Resisted, persisted, forced your way,
and tried your best
to untangle the knots in your chest.
You've swept so much of your heart
under rugs
that being walked over now feels familiar.

Some things just can't be buried deep enough.
Pain grows up and out from the mud,
little reminders resurfacing like weeds.
This was not the life you had imagined.
Some days you feel as if you're being crushed beneath undeserved burdens,
left wondering where you went wrong,
and how much more you can take.

Maybe it's time you stop punishing yourself further
for lessons already learned.
Maybe it's time you stop shrinking to fit within the frame
of others' expectations.
Maybe it's time for you to be the person you've been needing all along.
Maybe it's time for you to finally let go of the life you once envisioned,
and flow forward,
towards the one awaiting.

Living Rooms

I like seeing people's humanness.
Their little oddities and peculiarities.
The wallflowers too shy to shine,
and the ones consumed by the incomprehensible.
I like seeing the way people unfold slowly
and grow excited when you unlock the right door.
I like hearing people talk passionately
about things not everyone will appreciate.

We are made of much more
than simple living rooms.
There are attics and basements
and trap doors and nooks in each of us,
and I like being someone you know you can trust enough
to allow inside.
Play me your favorite songs – I want to hear them.
Tell me about the child still dancing across your heart
and what gives you butterflies.
What are you most proud of?
What's crushing you?

Because one thing I've learned is that almost none of us are ok.
Very few of us are fine.
We've been convinced nobody cares about what's killing us.
We keep our nightmares to ourselves.
We just do our job.
We just raise our children.
We just show up and smile.
We just try to focus on the positive.
But I know the way you ache.
I know how to cry quietly.
We're all a little broken.
We're all just fighting through things we weren't anticipating
and hanging on for dear life.
I hope you know you're never as alone as you might believe.
I hope you know I'm someone you can catch your breath beside.

More Importantly

There are things I want to give you
that I never had as a child.

Friendship – someone who will listen patiently
while you're still searching for your voice
and making sense of yourself.
Trust – someone you can confide in
when you're not sure who to turn to.
Affection – someone whose arms will forever be embracing.
Time & Attention – you will never have to fight for either.
Space – so that you may learn to fly and fall, succeed, and fail,
all on your own,
though never alone.
Consistency – today, tomorrow, every day, I will be there.
Safety – so long as I'm alive, I will fight for you,
I will protect and defend you.
And most of all, Love – with every ounce of my being, I will love you
unconditionally, always.
There is nothing you can do that could ever change that.

You may not know this, but you rescued me.
You became a beacon,
a lighthouse shining brightly and helping me find my way.
How blessed I am to help you find yours.

The very same things I'm giving you
seem to be healing me.

Transcendent

It's my belief that we were always meant to be.
We were written in the stars,
tethered from the start.
From the moment we met,
I knew it could only be you.
It's as if you breathed life into me.
The heart and soul sense connections
on levels deeper than we're meant to comprehend.
It's obvious there are parts of you and I which transcend logic.
Two hearts moving towards each other without us realizing it.
I like that what we share is entirely our own.
An unrivaled, unparallelled, unbreakable bond.
Speaking a language
only its counterpart understands.
We're an energy.
We're music and a vibration
and something bigger than either of us are individually.

I've learned that time spent in love is never wasted,
even while apart.
Everything leading up to us
was just as vital
as everything that happens moving forward,
now together.

I would go through it all again to be here with you.
I would wait lifetimes if that's what it took
for us to exist.
I carried you in my heart then.
I carry you in my heart now.
I carry you in my heart always.

Old Photos

I've come to accept that some of the grief
is coming with me.
Not everything haunting can be left behind
and forgotten.
Even long after I believe myself healed,
memories sneak up on my senses
and reopen old wounds.
I'm all scar tissue.

Some days, I just hide from the world.
And when someone tells me to focus on all the beautiful things instead,
I don't bother explaining to them that the beautiful things
are what's most difficult.

My grief hides in smiles, too.
My grief lives in laughter that sounds like those
I'll never hear again.
My grief takes road trips
and visits all our favorite places.
My grief celebrates every holiday.
My grief claps for me when nobody else
is there to.
My grief can't help but look through old photos
already burned into memory,
just to feel them again.

Because even if the only thing left to feel
is their absence,
it's better than not feeling them at all.
It's better than trying to forget someone
you know in your heart you never will.

The Real You

You're not who I thought.
The version you could only pretend to be
was the person you knew I needed.

My God,
I fought so hard for something so empty.
All I did was break myself into pieces
trying to find ones you'd keep.
All I did was wonder why I wasn't enough.
I'm not even mad anymore.
I know this is pointless.
The truth always tastes like poison to liars.
Manipulation is only justifiable to the gutless.
It's never narcissism in the eyes of those
who can't see anything wrong with themselves.
The most insecure can't stomach their own weakness,
so they feed off others' strengths.

I know you hate your reflection,
so brag about the masks.
Rise early in the morning
without ever waking up
and decide which one to wear tomorrow.
Then step out into a world that will always seem cold
when the fake you
is the real you.

Yes To Myself

Perhaps one of the most painful experiences I've had to learn
is how to fall out of love
with the *idea* I had of others.
That what I hoped to come true
in a few I cared deepest for,
never will.
That promise and potential
are only hypothetical,
and I've accepted less than I deserve
for long enough.

I'm moving forward.
On a path now, and no longer a loop.

It took me quite some time to realize
only I can assert my own worth.
I've stifled my spirit and bit my tongue bloody.
I've bent to the whims of others for so long that standing up for myself
now seems defiant.
The only thing more satisfying than saying *"no"*
to someone who never appreciated my sacrifice in the first place,
is saying *"yes"* to myself.

This isn't starting over
because I'm not going back.
I reduced myself to something that made you feel bigger
than you ever actually were.
It's not just that I've outgrown you,
I've outgrown the version of me
you could control.

Wherever We Go

Let us step into each new day together,
with a sense of awe and excitement,
and no fear of the future.
Let's hold tightly to one another
while walking gratefully down roads
all our own.
Let's appreciate the magic
within each moment shared
and make a million memories worth revisiting.

This is our once in a lifetime.
This is our never-ending crescendo.
This is our masterpiece in the making.

On difficult days meant to test us,
let's remember to draw towards one another,
and never away.
Seasons change
and harsh weather is temporary.
The love and bond we share
will always be our greatest strength.
You are my biggest inspiration.
The *"Yes We Can!"*
following any doubt or question.
The meaning and reason
hidden in every message.
And all I will ever need in life.

Wherever we go, we are always home.

Beginnings of Endings

Just give her some space.
A little room to stretch and catch her breath.
A moment to reflect
and take in her surroundings.
All of this is unfamiliar.

Black hearts tend to relapse,
returning to the places tearing them apart.
People are a drug,
and some are poison.
Murderous to the best of us.
The diamond shining brightest
also blinds us from the slicing.

It's difficult when someone you trusted
becomes the reason you question your own judgement.

A seed of doubt, now with roots
she's struggling to pull out.

Just give her some space to sew herself back up.
To stop the bleeding.
To sweep away the pieces no longer needed.
To uncover her confidence.
To shine on her own again.
A moment to return to the heart of herself.
She's learning to love in all new ways -
from beginnings of endings.
There's so much pain in the breaking,
but there's beauty in the mending.

J. Raymond

Let Me Know You Made It Home

This morning,
while drinking my coffee at the little shop on the corner,
I saw a woman shrink.
Her gait doubled in pace
as she passed a group of men standing around their work truck.
Pulling elbows, handbag, and shoulders, into herself.
Lowering her head and gaze,
as if hoping to be invisible.

Once inside the coffee shop, without thinking,
she quickly locked the door behind her.

And in that moment,
I believe I saw what trauma looks like.
I saw habits formed by a fear
that's never followed me home.
She turned around,
embarrassed
and face blushing as red as a STOP sign
with the word PLEASE written above it,
checking to see if anyone noticed.
I did.
Averting eye contact and looking away again,
she unlocks the door, shrinks a little more
and hides in line, waiting to place her order.

I wanted to tell her it's ok,
that I'm not going to hurt her,
but that sounded in my head like the kind of thing
someone threatening would say.
So, I just left.
And on my way home
I crossed the street before getting too close to anybody else.
Not because I felt unsafe,
but because I didn't want them to.

For whatever it's worth,
you don't need to be invisible around me.
For whatever it's worth,
I'll watch the door.

Apology Accepted

I owe myself an apology.
For all the times I promised to forgive myself,
only to bring it up again later.
For clipping the wings of my own dreams
before they ever had a chance to take flight.
For thinking so little of myself
at the very moments I should have been standing up for myself.
For the lies I swallowed
while starving for truth.
For believing that all the glass I walked on as a child
was ever my fault.
For withholding the same grace and second chances
I so freely give others.
For allowing the world to convince me that my heart
was both too much
and not enough.
For all the days wasted
pretending to be someone you would accept.
For not living life more on my own terms,
simply because I was afraid of making a mistake.
For punishing myself for far too long.
For believing love was blood-soaked and painful,
and that I didn't deserve better.
For every time I looked in the mirror
and hated who I saw.

I could sit here listing every reason and way
I was wronged by others,
but maybe more than anything,
I owe myself an apology for not valuing this one,
beautifully precious life of mine enough to know
I'm worthy of greatness,
the very best of everything.

And for that, I am sorry.

This Was The Year

This is neither the end, nor the beginning.
The year I finally found appreciation
in my failings.
I can look back at the way everything unfolded
and see that I was never snake-bitten.
The way I broke was necessary.
I said goodbye to a few who left
when I needed them most
and discovered self-reliance.

Even the most perfect gifts
may be agonizing to unpackage.

When you're in the depths of hell itself,
it's so hard to see the blessing it will become.
Somedays,
it takes everything you have just to survive.
To keep going,
not knowing how you'll pull yourself from this nightmare.
Yet you do.
You make it to morning
and the sunlight starts hitting you a bit differently.
You're changing. Growing again.
Believing that, against all odds,
the things you want most are closer to you
by virtue of everything you've gone through.

This year I understood the significance
of every misstep.
That perfection is impossible,
and how even the heartbreaks I never saw coming
were always meant to find me.
This was the year I learned acceptance.
This was the year I learned everything needed
exists inside me already.

Found In The Dark

It almost always comes back to instincts.
Listening to the hushed whispers only she can hear.
Then believing in what her heart already knows to be true.

Knowing what to pursue
and what needs to be set free,
isn't always easy.
How are we sure what to continue fighting for,
and what we must give up on?

She would never be someone who walks away
from what she loves
unscathed.
Sometimes staying is painful
but letting go leaves scars.

Deep within
were shelves lined with books
both old and new, filled with stories
she thought would never end.
Miles of aisles she still walks down
some nights.
Even the ones hurtful to read are necessary.
It's impossible to forget the reasons she changed.
It sticks to fingertips.
When she turns over new pages
it leaves a print.
A part of what made her, what shaped her,
travels into a future she believes
will be brighter.

It's amazing how far some must go
to find their way back.
Her soul made a home with the pieces
discovered in the dark.

Still Shining

I could allow the grief to bury me alive.
Just let the loss of you
crush whatever's left of me.

But you're not a memory.
You're a light still shining.
Burning bright, something I carry with me.

When I speak of you,
I do so without remorse.
I beam with pride.
I speak of your exuberance.
I give them your energy.
I tell them you were art embodied.
Dancing avant-garde, bold and beautiful.
Where you went, sunshine followed.
I tell them that you made life musical.
Every smile, a celebration.
Every laugh, a song.

Your life, your light,
changed me in the greatest of ways.
All the love shared between us doesn't cease
simply because you're not beside me.
You're within me.
My skin and bones.
My heart and soul.
The air I breathe.
The sun I stand beneath.
You are all around.
You are everything that made me.
That sort of light never fades.

I'll take all the love we shared,
and continue sharing it.

Threadbare

Your heart is not an inconvenience.
It's incredibly brave to believe in good things,
to keep your world wide-open and welcoming.
Kindness is often manipulated and taken for granted.
Empathy is exploited,
hunted and fed upon
by the soul-sick and hopeless.

You give and give and give,
until whatever protective layers remain
grow threadbare.
You're wearing thin.
You're pouring into a bottomless well.
Screaming into unrelenting headwinds.
Swimming upstream nowhere,
waiting for tides to turn that never will.
Takers take because they have little of value to offer.

But know this - the love you deserve
will never be empty-handed.
It'll multiply everything it touches.

You'll ask for a moment,
and they'll stop time for you.
It will be both abundant and considerate.
Life becomes an adventure to enjoy,
not something you endure.

When you're used to abuse,
someone loving you gently
almost seems too good to be true.
Maybe all those seeds you've sown have grown.

They just might not be where you were expecting.

Best Of You

I want to smile again, without feeling guilty.
I want to miss you, without coming undone.
I want to celebrate your life,
without my heart breaking.

If there's a good side of grief, I've yet to reach it.
It's not getting any easier.
Time isn't helping.
Some days I feel as if the pain only deepens.
The roads ahead seem longer without you walking them beside me.
It's like I'm resistant to joy.
Pushing back against my own happiness.
I'm afraid that healing means forgetting,
and I'm not ready to leave.
Let me sit here for a little while longer.
There are things I needed to tell you
that I never got the chance to.
Things you deserved to hear....

I'm sorry.
I'm sorry for not doing more.
If it were possible to bear your pain,
I would have.
Even when distant, my world was better because you were in it.
I was always proud of you.
My love for you is constant,
unconditional, eternal.
There are pieces of you I'm discovering in me.
Little gifts you unknowingly left behind.
Even your absence is filled with moments worth revisiting.

Maybe instead of learning how to live without you,
I'll just bring the best of you with me.
Maybe we're not meant to move on,
we're meant to move with.

Take This For The Pain

I didn't understand how much it would hurt to heal.
I thought I'd be further along by now.
A bit more intact.

Some days, I float weightless
atop my grief.
Allow it to carry me freely wherever.
And others,
I'm pulled into the cold, endless depths of it.
Wave after wave of reminders and memories.
I thought by now I'd be stronger.
I'd be able to swim out from the undertow
and breathe again.
I didn't understand how much of me is missing without you.
I feel lost.
I'm tired of condolences and well wishes.
I want to laugh with you again.
I want to see you walk through the door.
I want to hear your footsteps coming toward me once more.
I didn't understand how quiet life would be without you here.
There's only echoes now.
I call out and wait for a reply I know
isn't coming.
I didn't understand how much of my heart
was home for you.
I'm filled with empty spaces
I'm not sure what to do with now.
How much can one person lose
before there's nothing left of themselves?
I just didn't understand how much it would hurt
to heal.

Wildflowers Within Me

I'm not always strong.
I don't have it all together.
I squint and can't always see the light
at the end of the tunnel I'm stuck inside.

Even though I know there's plenty
to be grateful for,
my heart gets so heavy at times.
My arms shake from holding myself together.
I want to believe in something again.
I want to learn whatever lessons are hidden
in all this hurt.
I want to understand why I'm here
and they aren't.
I'm tired of being in pieces.
I'm tired of pretending everything is fine.
I'm tired of stepping into grief like quicksand.
The harder I fight, the faster I sink,
and I'm not sure what or who
I'm even fighting for anymore.
I'm loosely stitched together
with nothing but hopes and dreams,
and I'm tearing at the seams.
As much as I tell myself to be tough,
some days,
all I do is fall apart.
There are wildflowers within me I meant to give you,
and they're wilting now that you're gone.
They bloom whenever I remember
to water them,
and I know you'd only want me to smile.
You'd only want me to be happy.
You'd tell me all the flowers were meant for me.

All You Know

It took time to find sunlight.
To accept that the darkest parts of my life
also needed grieving

It was never my own shadow I was afraid of.
And maybe it was never that I stopped trying.
as much as I just got used to hurting.
When all you know is trauma,
you start to anticipate pain.
You don't flinch at anything dangerous.
A part of you starts believing that blood from love and abuse
flow from the same vein.
You make homes in places
you ought to run from.

It took time to realize that you can't let go
of what you refuse to feel.
And maybe it was never that I expected my life to be easy,
as much as I couldn't understand why those closest
were the ones crushing me.
When all you know is chaos,
you learn to sense energy.
The slightest shift in tone
or change in temperature
never goes unnoticed.

It took time to find sunlight.
To trust that it wouldn't burn me.
To let it warm my soul.
I feel like I was so busy just trying to survive
that I'm only now getting a chance to live.

Real Life Magic

It's really quite simple – in every imaginable way,
my life is better because you're in it.

You're such a gift to my spirit.
It's never lost on me how lucky I am.
Your love has taught me
how to better love myself.
There's a piece to the puzzle that,
once in place,
brings the picture into focus.
You're that piece for me.
Even though we can't predict the future,
I know we're in it together.
I see forever in us.
You're my coffee in bed and how I want to begin every day,
for the rest of my life.
Long walks together are adventures.
We're real-life magic.
Something extraordinary.
Every moment made more colorful and memorable with you in it.
You're my confidence and confidant.
My backbone and resilience.
And when the storms of life roll in,
I know we're safe within the walls we've built.
I know that whatever hardships are thrown our way,
we'll only grow closer.
We only overcome.
You're the best part of my life.
The heartbeat of everything.
It was always you. It could only ever be you.

It's really quite simple – in every imaginable way,
my life is better because you're in it.

Do You Understand

I'm stubborn,
which means I dig my heels deeply in places
I should be avoiding.
I'll apologize too late,
and then beat myself up long after
you've forgiven me.

I'm an overthinker,
which means I've already considered
every worst-case scenario.
And because I was raised in a home
I never felt safe in,
I've already located the nearest exit –
keeping in mind it may be behind me.
My anxiety makes it difficult to meet
and keep friends.
Honestly, I don't even feel like I'm good
to the few I have.

I'm so hard on myself that I've forgotten how to celebrate victories,
and when people tell me I should be proud,
the words *"for what?"* follow behind it like an anchor.
Have you ever hurt yourself because there was nowhere left to store the pain?
I hoped by now I'd have learned
how to be kind to myself without feeling foolish.
When asked the question *"are you happy?"*,
I always answer incorrectly.
Because when I am, I'm not sure I should be.
And when I'm not, I feel guilty.

Do you understand?

Star Crossed

This pain will pass,
but it's taking some of me with it.
I won't be the same after you.
The most significant people may only be here for a moment.
The impression they leave upon your heart, however,
is something permanent.

We were always star-crossed.
Even with half your heart,
you showed me a love brighter
and more ablaze
than any love I'd ever known.

But I also know I deserve someone's everything.
Their entirety.
I refuse to settle for good
when I know great is waiting.
As cruel as fate may be,
I don't consider us a failure.
We will always be necessary
to one another's story.

It's clear to me now -
you were brought into my life to teach me
the art of letting go.
You don't always get to keep
everything you love.
But everything you love
keeps a piece of you.

Let It Fall

Not all my tears are weighed down heavy
and heart-wrenching.
Some roll warmly down my cheeks,
collecting along the curved corners
of my smile.
More like a sun shower
reaching and reviving old roots.

You give me life.

I cry because I miss you terribly.
But I also cry because the memories I hold close
are so beautiful.
Both are cleansing.
Both are necessary to each other.
Grief is what love leaves behind.
Gifts we're grateful to open,
painful they may be.

My favorite memories are threads
fed through the eyelets of needles
used to stitch myself back together.
Remembering you is coalescing,
though only for a moment.
And because I know grief rains down forever,
I will let it soak me to the bone.
I will learn to dance in its heaviness.
I will find you in the middle of every storm.

Now That I Do

I like how the moon is sometimes visible
during the day.

It makes me feel like I, too,
can shine somewhere other than in darkness.

I'm still working to ensure everything I went through
was worth it.
Otherwise, it's just wasted pain.
My goal now is to be seen *completely*,
not *completed*.
I've broken too many times to ever be whole.

Maybe that's where I went wrong –
I gave one person everything,
and every other person
nothing.

It's amazing how far one can go without believing in themselves.
I wonder where I'll wind up now that I do.
One thing I'm sure of – I can do it alone.
I know how to fall in places
nobody will catch me.
I know how to grow
from rock bottom,
where light may not reach.

Maybe it wasn't love I was chasing,
as much as it was memories
I was erasing.
In the end,
I'll make sure all the pain
wasn't in vain.

Deathly Things

There are a million swirling emotions
coursing through me.
Always.

Some days, I'm overwhelmed with inspiration.
The entire world seems to speak to me,
beckoning me to be swallowed up whole by it.

So, I let it.

The tides lap at my ankles,
trying to tug me into the unknown.
I'm terrified with excitement.
I'm amazed by my desire to feel lost.
There's a labyrinth in me,
and I just want to run wildly through it,
alongside somebody brave.
Somebody patient.
Who sees the squalor of my heart
like abstract art.
Who hears everything in my head as music,
not noise.
Who accepts me as a complexity,
not a problem needing solving.

Even deathly things are rearranged and made beautiful
in the right hands.

Losing You, Finding Me

You weren't listening
when I said we were hemorrhaging.
When I said I'd rather live with the pain of missing you
than live with the way you break me.

Please don't act surprised.
Our ending stretched for miles.
The death of us was far from abrupt.
Now we're out of road.
We're out of rope.
All our chances used up.
In the end,
manipulating me
was easier than fixing yourself.
I should've chosen myself long ago.
You never cared that I was drowning.
Only blamed me
while pulling us down further.
Turns out there's more than one way
someone can take your breath away.

We've got to save ourselves from ourselves now.
You're safer as a stranger.
What hurts is that every way for me to heal and find happiness again
includes losing you.
The only place for you in my life
is in my past.
We were meant to be.
Just not meant to last.

With You Always

As you move through life, take each step excitedly,
knowing how much you are loved.
Knowing there's at least one person out there who believes in you
with every fiber of their being.

To me, you are the entire world.
In your eyes I see strength that has pushed me
through my own tough times.
I see a universe filled with endless opportunities
just waiting for you to grab hold of them.
I see someone worthy and deserving of the very best of everything.
If ever you doubt yourself, turn to me.
I will show you everything within you I know to be true.
I will show you the force that you are,
and every reason to keep fighting.
And on the days you just need someplace safe to rest,
I hope you know that I will be there to rest with you, too.

You've given me strength when weak,
and direction when lost.
You're the reason I never quit,
the reason I continue to dream.
Wherever you decide to go,
know that I am always with you.
Just as you are always with me.
You are never alone.

Atop Our Graves

Thank you for never giving up.
We each had our own wars to fight
en route to one another.
It feels like a miracle,
being here with you.

If I could,
I'd go back in time
and meet you in the middle of every catastrophe.
I'd sit beside you
at the bottom of your lowest moments,
just to keep you company.
A million different scenarios had to unfold
the exact way they did,
for us to exist.

I wonder how many times we both noticed
the same quartered moon,
while the weight of another night crushed us.
Nothing is an accident.
We had to break a few times before we were ready
to love each other properly.
Every setback strengthened us.
What a gift our failures became.

Gardens grew atop our graves,
until we were ready to breathe again.

Thank you for surviving.
For blossoming in every way
that now saves me daily.
We would not be here, if not for you.
If I could,
I'd go back in time and let you know
I'm fighting, too.

Keep The Tree Up

Leave the Christmas tree up because it makes you happy.
(That's a good enough reason.)
Spend the day guilt-free in bed
with the shades drawn.
(Justification isn't necessary.)
Ignore phone calls when you don't have the energy needed.
(Don't defend yourself.)

Some days,
I'll listen to all the sad songs on repeat
because I don't have to fake how I feel.

Our truths must only be honest,
not positive.

I can't hide anymore.
There are parts of who I am
I'm not proud of.
Pretending they don't exist
only made me sick.
It only took away from my peace.

We've got to start loving what we already have,
and who we already are,
on the way to whoever we're becoming.
Find joy in the mundane.
Embrace your oddities.
Go where you're watered.
Grow where others love to lift you.
Act childish, be kind, mind your business,
and smile.
Because the thrill *is* life,
and the ride is short.

Unscathed

She never expected perfection.
Only someone steady.
Someone courageous,
who'd withstand the rough weather
and not run from thunder.
Someone who appreciates the price paid to fall.
Who would ride out the storm
and see through her scars.
Who respects the parts of her
needing a gentle touch and patience.

Love hasn't always been kind.
It's been abusive and neglectful.
Left her abandoned, bruised,
and questioning herself.
Please understand that the thing she longs for also frightens her.
Though she believes in the timing of everything,
she's aware of how much she'll never get back,
and knows better than to waste any more of it.
The most beautiful things in life can turn ugly quickly.

She never expected more than she'd give.
Only someone who truly knew
what it meant to commit.
Who would reassure her when worried.
Who loved her thoroughly, wildly, consistently.
Who didn't come to her needing to be saved.
Who recognized she went through hell,
yet didn't survive it unscathed.

Gentle Sparks

I won't stand for mediocre love.
I want my knees buckling.
I want love to swallow me up like storm clouds.
Roll over me with its warm grey
and let me fall like rain.
I want love to rinse me clean and shock me.
I want love to be thrilling yet reassuring.
I want to curl up with it in front of a fire
and lose track of time.
I want to make a world beneath our sheets.
A universe no one else can see.
I want our feet and bare skin
brushing against the others.
Gentle sparks setting fire
to hearts hidden behind the softest barbed wire.
I want the taste of your lips atop my tongue,
and that wild, rampant hair across my face.
I want your bated breath, arching back,
and every curvature.
I want your love coursing through me.
I want to be awestruck by you forever.
I want to love you in every way you've prayed for.
I want the love we've been waiting on our entire lives.

There are things in life best enjoyed in doses
and small moderation –
but *this* is not one of them.
I refused a lackluster love,
and the world brought me you - a brilliant wildfire.
And now there's not a single part of everything you are
that I could ever live without.

This Is Wholeness

If all you have for me is war,
take it elsewhere.
I've got gunpowder in my guts,
fire in my eyes.
arrows in my spine,
and I'm through fighting.

Bring me your pieces and I'll bring you peace.

I've survived so much that I'm still
sorting through my own remains.
Plotting new courses,
redesigning my dreams,
learning each of my boundaries.
Seeing who's still beside me.
I've spent so much of my life in battle
that I'm looking forward to stillness.

I can tell you
when you've been abused for long enough,
hurting seems easier than healing.
No matter how I rearrange myself,
I'm incomplete.
I'm a million heroes and monsters
and not nearly enough forgiveness.
But what if everything they took,
everything missing that I'll never get back,
is room needed for whatever's left to grow?
Because one thing's for sure -
it took a lot of loss for me to feel this whole.

Long Before I Found Myself

Most of my life I've felt alone,
even while in the company of others.
I bent and acquiesced until emptied.
Me in pain was never upsetting enough for them
to cease being the cause.
I'd cut myself open and dig for something of value.
Something they might deem worthy.
Something they'd be proud to keep.

It's easy to ruminate on what I could've done differently.
But our paths are our paths, and the timing of it all
rarely makes sense.
The person I am today
only exists because of who I used to be.
There was heart racing fear
long before I found bravery.
My bones shook with anxiousness
before I walked with confidence.
Hardships brought about humility,
and shame preceded pride.
It's only because I know suffering
that I'm able to thoroughly appreciate peace.

I've come too far to not be happy.
I'll smile for no reason and find joy in places
others don't think to look.
Whatever good there is in my world,
please know that I earned it.
There's a gift hidden in grief.
Pain becomes strength,
and falling is never failing when the gift
is discovering your own resilience.

I Will Be The One

I want to be the one who breaks the chain.
The last link.
Where all the trauma ends and the cycle stops.
I want to be the one
who makes it out of the woods alive
and shows you the way.
Who defies the odds,
rewrites their future,
becomes a new example to follow.
I want to be the one
who passes compassion on to the next generation,
not agony.
Who extends an open, loving hand,
not a cold, closed fist.
The one who creates a world for my children
far safer than the one I knew.
I want to be the one who uplifts and listens.
The birdsong after a storm.
The beacon.
The first person you think to turn to.
The flare in the sky you look for.
The haven you run to.

It stops here – the habit of suffering.
I will remove the rot by the roots.
Violence will not be handed down.
Hurting is not hereditary.
I will not break others
simply to feed on their pieces.
I will heal for the sake of us all.
Pain will not be perpetuated.
Love will be my legacy.
I will be the one.

I swear it...
I will be the one.

Living Lyrically

Nothing will ever move me like music.

The right song is a balm, soothing the soul.
Music sat beside me through my worst hells
and consoled me.
Pulled me from the depths of myself
and offered both hope and empathy.

When rage was needed, it screamed.
And when I thought nobody could possibly understand my pain,
music let me weep.

The right lyric, at the right time,
will lift my spirits in ways only nature understands.
It seems there's a soundtrack to every season of life.
Some bring me back in time to better days.
Others remind me of how far I've come.

What's most exciting is the notion that,
just as I've yet to meet all the people who might love me,
I've not yet discovered all the music that will speak to me.

It's the remedy for most every ailment,
mending what people break.
Every moment within every day has a score.
Maybe all the noise in my head and heart
have been songs all along.
And I'm only now learning what to listen for.

Love The Lie

Sometimes the only thing holding us together
is the hope I feel slipping through my fingers.

I thought our story would read differently.
I thought I saw the way we'd become one.
My God,
are we fools for trying?
It's so hard to tell the difference
between stubbornness and persistence.
Despite time and distance,
I always feel your presence.
We're connected, still tethered together.
I'm ok with not knowing how it ends.
Maybe I just like believing in something that feels real.

Maybe one day I'll let go.
I'll *really* let go and leave us to history.
But whenever I get close to quitting,
I tell myself that even a small piece of you
is better than nothing at all.
I tell myself that I deserve more,
only to look you in the eyes
and see that you're everything.
There's space in my heart you occupy,
but I keep the windows and doors open now.

The truth is,
hoping we find our way back to one another
hurts a lot less than *accepting* we never will.

Please, Make Yourself Comfortable

My anxiety made me unacceptable to myself.
Every self-revelation and reflection
torn down and judged with disgust.
So, I wore masks carefully crafted with patches
borrowed from everybody else.

My anxiety made me unwelcome in my own skin.
Most of my life I've been running to places
I'd soon need to run from.
Home was always wherever I wasn't.

My anxiety wants me lost and confined
at the same time.
Boxed in behind windowless walls, one day.
Hopping one-way trains, the next.
It tells me that the only things you'll see in me
are the very things I'm trying to hide.

My anxiety kept the real me quieted for so long
that I forgot the sound of my own laugh.
My anxiety pushes me to work hard towards a goal
I'll later tell myself
I'm undeserving of.

You see,
the real work is breaking out of your own cage
and setting yourself free.

The truth - I'm more love than hate,
more hope than despair,
more light than darkness,
and even on my worst days
I can find something to smile about.
I've survived a hundred horrors already.
All that's left of me is faith.
I've built a home within me
where every version is welcomed.

Everything Was Vibrant

I don't need to know.
I don't have all the answers.
I don't even care where we go from here, so long as it's together.

What if we just chose to float freely...
Without aim.
Without the end in mind.
Without the weight of expectations
holding us down.
What if we just watered one another -
blossomed and grew roots.
What if we got out of the way,
and allowed fate to unfold before us?

Something brought us together.
You feel it, too – this connection.
This energy and pull towards one another.
It seems almost otherworldly.
One moment my life was recognizable, familiar.
Then, suddenly,
everything was vibrant.
Now I can't look back.
It's taken a lifetime to trust what touches me deeply.

Even though I don't always understand it,
I owe it to my soul to make the most of this journey.
It's easy to overlook the future
when the space you're in
feels like everything.
If forever never arrives, please know
this will still be enough for me.

Long Nights

Letting go isn't always a loss.
It seems the only way to find out what you're made of
is by being ripped open.
I've lost count of the stars that have spilled out of me
wasted on the empty wishes of others.
Now I grow my own dreams.
The only way to evolve
is imperfectly.
I'm an amalgamation of messy things.
Like a full moon and the fiery sun
hidden behind ominous skies –
I burn and shine bright
even when nobody sees me.
I've been through too much
to stay anywhere loveless.
I've seen too much
to walk through life blindly.
I'll feel my way out.
My most valuable traits
earned through painful lessons learned.
I'm both sides of the coin.
Made of good and evil,
dreams and nightmares.
I've buried my burdens.

The further I go,
the more peace I find in acceptance –
not everything that ends is a failure.

So, in a way, I'm grateful for the pain.
If I could go back and do it all differently,
I wouldn't.
I'm proud of my path,
and the corrections made along the way.
Even when I'm not where I thought I'd be,
I'm always right where I'm meant to be.

One Final Time

I'm aware of the risk.
I know the feeling of giving everything to another
and it never being enough.
I know the sullen sound of letdown.
I know how endings arrive angrily and fanged.
Even knowing we might strike hurtful chords in one another,
I will choose us.
I will wrap us in compassion,
and respect that we're a dangerous thing
because we're a wounded thing.

We could have continued walking life alone.
We could have remained hidden,
free from expectations
and safe from disappointment.
Yet, here we stand,
with whatever is left of two beaten hearts.
You found me somewhere I kept to myself.
With the curtains closed tight,
growing just fine in lonesome places
making my own light.

And despite the likelihood of being hurt again,
I will love you.
I will open myself wholly,
knowing I'm exposed to the elements
and that one-day winter will arrive.
I will wait with you patiently for Spring
in the hopes that this will be our season of receiving.
I will not leave when I'm afraid.
I will stay when it isn't easy.
I will strive to see us through.
I will appreciate the parts of us both
that have been devalued and overlooked.
For you,
for myself,
I will lay it all on the line
one final time.

This Is How You Love Yourself

Loving yourself begins with showing up as yourself.
Display your individuality, unapologetically.
Wear every imperfection.

Don't hide what you've healed –
the world needs to know.
Proudly present the skewed, disheveled, disorderly YOU.
Authenticity doesn't guarantee acceptance.
Some won't like the way you shine,
sight unseen.
Without ever knowing your soul,
they'll make up their minds about who you are.
Having never walked your roads,
overcome your obstacles,
learned your lessons,
they'll form their own conclusions and judge your journey.
So what.

Let your greatest strength be an outright refusal to allow
the opinions and treatment from others
to dictate your own behavior.
Treat yourself with kindness, love, and affection,
even when someone else decides you don't deserve it.

There's magic beneath your surface,
but not everyone will unearth it.
Beauty endures with depth.
Love yourself so wildly those in your presence
begin demanding more from themselves.
I hope anyone struggling to see their own light
turns towards yours and grows.

New Futures

We can make something from this.
We can break back into place.
We can turn this falling apart into art.

Let's just throw the wheel in a different direction.
Let's go somewhere we've never been before.
And paint new futures
overtop these old backdrops.
Let's build another foundation altogether.
Let's reinvent ourselves
and the love we share.
We're not done yet.
I won't watch us wash away into gray.
You are still my brightest light.
The very sun and stars
in an otherwise dark space.

I'm sorry for ever making you feel alone.
For those nights that swallowed you whole.
I never wanted you to have to fight for peace.
Or to pine for the very best
buried inside me.

Some of what we're outrunning
moves us away from one another.
Forgive me for not being there.
The further I go,
the more I'm brought back to what matters most -
You.
I hope our future is so beautiful
that we won't need to look back on our tough times to laugh.

We could lose everything
and still have the world,
so long as we have one another.

Something Like A Sycamore

Here's what she said –

"I'm tired of doing it all alone.
Though I'm able to appreciate all the beauty in my world,
I can't help but wonder how much more it would mean
to witness it alongside someone safe.
Someone I'm certain of.
Someone kindhearted
who I could count on,
and who could count on me.
This desire doesn't stem from desperation, however.
Please know, I'm not afraid of fending for myself.
I've already proven to myself that I can.
My own company isn't something I dread or need escaping from.
I'm content with the way each day blooms beneath my feet
and carries me easily into the next.
But I'd love to laugh more with someone I could call mine.
Someone who appreciates everything I've gone through
to be everything they need.
I hope for intimacy with another that makes the normalcy of life feel magical.
I want to see things through the eyes of someone inspiring.
Slow, peaceful days spent with someone who knows I'm wonderful
just
   as
    I
     am.
See, I'm strong alone, something like a Sycamore tree in an open field.
I feel the rain, sun, breeze, and am truly grateful
for each passing season.
But it sure would be nice to have someone who just loves sitting beside me.
Someone to bask beside."

Safekeeping

I've let go so many times that my hands
aren't sure what to hold.
Fists, tired of fighting, slowly unfurling,
like two peonies held in front me.
I want to keep the beauty for myself this time,
I think,
and make sure it's safe.

I've returned to painful places so many times
that peaceful ones feel unsettling.
Love bent me without forgiveness.
Brought me to my knees,
genuflecting out of fear.
I've made myself silent and small
in homes that were once warm,
because I was shown that not all love
is welcoming.
Not all love is uplifting.
I've tip-toed and peeked around corners
searching for monsters I was told I deserved.
Monsters who loved the way I'd break beneath them.

I had to quit that which was killing me.
I had to run and hide from the ones I once leapt towards.
I had to sweep up the pieces of a soul
needing to become its own home.
Quitting the forever I imagined
so the one destined could exist.
Now there's laughter on my lips.
Hope,
no longer caught in my throat.

I'm still holding beauty loosely in my hands,
only,
I'm no longer silent.
I may have lost my way
but I found my voice.

Welcome & Worthy

I hope my smile is something like a neon sign that reads:

Even when I don't understand what you're going through,
I care about you.
Even when you feel unrecognizable,
I see you.
When the voices in your head are deafening,
I will listen to you.
I may not know your trauma,
but I'll try like hell to hear what's hardest to say.
Let's laugh at the mistakes and heartbreaks we have in common.
And if you're tired of holding it all together,
feel free to fall apart.
I don't know your fears and the wickedness you've witnessed.
I don't know your hardships,
and how you chose to cope.
I don't know the horrors you hold close.

Do not apologize for the sadness
that sometimes shadows your shine.
Stop watering the seeds of doubt
planted in you by others.
Stop judging yourself solely on your worst decisions –
you're not even that person anymore.
Stop hurting yourself over the pain others have already inflicted.
Forgive your tolerance.
Forgive yourself.
You are loved.
You are needed.

Look at what you made from hurricanes.
Your survival was no accident.
You took the hardest parts of life
and were made softer by them.
Who would you be without your tragedies?

I don't know how else to say
every version you are is welcomed here.
You've always been worthy.

Wildflower Honey

I'm saying "*yes*" to life.
I want the sweetness of it
dripping from my lips like wildflower honey.
I want to sink my teeth into fleshy fruit
and feel its juices run down my arms and elbows.
I want my toes to curl beneath weighty passion,
so jolting it's an awakening.
I feel alive again, reinvigorated.
Reborn with purpose.
I was asleep, my spirit dormant.
Settling for the scraps and slices of life
when I should have been indulging.
I'm somewhere I never thought I'd be,
and I'm going to make the most of it.

I'm not sad for failing.
I'm not sorry for trying.
I'm not down on my knees.
I'm standing, arms stretched out wide and chest up high.
I'm an adventurer, a wanderer,
in love with the ethereal.
I'm not even on the same old roads anymore.
I'm carving a new trail altogether.
Going everywhere and nowhere
and offering my heart to others along the way.

I'm living, breathing, divinity.
My feet,
barely on the ground now.
I won't look down.
I won't look back.
And I won't wonder "what if".
I'll appreciate my path,
move on from what was,
and fall in love with what is.

Bring Me My Karma

And now it's clear - you can't save anyone.
I'm tired of mourning the parts of my heart
given freely to others.
Let me rest in pieces.
Sometimes,
the ones most in need of love,
may also be the least deserving of it.
Watering others until I wilted,
and emptying my cup.
Knowing yours overflowing
would never be enough.

There's so much love spilling out of me
that it must look for low points.
Deep ravines and voids that need filling.
Sometimes,
empathy is the enemy.
Bleeding out for those unwilling to heal themselves.
What causes me the most pain
is also what I'm most proud of -
    focusing on the good in others.

Though, finally
the tides have turned internally.
I'm nobody's caregiver.
I'm nobody's failsafe.
Don't come to me expecting rescue.
Come to me readied and intact.
Come to me open, not broken.
Bring your energy and passion,
and I will multiply it.
Bring me my karma.
Be my missing piece,
    not another puzzle.
Be sunlight and water
    to a flourishing garden.
A single, unbothered vine thrives
and climbs walls.
Either we'll grow wildly together,
or not at all.

Receive It

There are silver linings to painful lessons.
Beauty beyond our suffering.
Growth in the grieving.
Ultimately,
we mourn the life we imagined
while searching for peace in the present.

When winds of adversity beat down,
every step ahead is earned.
We take it in faith.
We push through our own exhaustion,
broken bones and spirit,
deeper, further into treacherous weather
unsure what awaits us,
and certain we are no longer the person we once were.

There are times we reach the fork in the road
and the direction we go
no longer feels like a choice.
Fate unfolds at our feet
and leads us down unfamiliar streets.
We're thrust into a reality far different
than the one we had envisioned.

Even if this isn't where I thought I'd be,
I will make it beautiful.
I'll stand atop the obstacles I once stumbled over.
I'll run with no end in mind.
I'll fall in love with life again,
because every day is a gift.
How I receive it,
   depends on how I perceive it.

Fall For No Reason

You asked how I knew you were the one....

And so,
I try explaining the weight of a million moments meant for me,
finally arriving,
and how badly I want to hold onto each.

I try explaining how you've altered my chemistry,
and now much of who I am
are made from what you saw in me.

I try explaining that your love is a light I always leave on,
and how it reminds me I'm never alone
in this home.

I try explaining the evolution of a miracle,
and how freeing it is to believe in someone other than myself.

I try explaining every instance your kindness has pulled me out
of my own darkness,
and how much strength exists in your grace.

I try explaining that waking up beside the person I waited and prayed for
makes every day a dream.

I try explaining what happens to my heart every time I feel your fingers
intertwine with mine,
and how it's the closest thing to perfection I've ever felt.

I wish I could tell you the moment I knew
you were the one for me,
but they're countless, immeasurable, never-ending.
You exhale and I catch my breath.
You laugh, and I fly.
You get dressed and I unravel.

As you live and breathe,
I find another reason to fall.

Then,
fall for no reason at all.

Don't Pick The Flowers

My boundaries are set like a white picket fence.
One that took years to build.
I constructed it high enough for me,
and low enough for you.
It's meant to be welcoming, though not for everybody.
These boundaries are for me.
It's me delineating the exact amount of respect I deserve.
It's me saying to the world, *"I value who I've become"*.
I hope when someone walks by, they see love on the other side
and realizes it grew from rock bottom.
You can fall a great distance
quicker than it will take to stand back up.

There were times I just needed someone to believe in me when I couldn't.
And when they never arrived, I went on alone.
There were times when I waited and waited and waited to catch a break.
And when it never arrived, I caught myself.
I rebuilt and healed myself.
I forgave myself for falling,
then accepted that I was deserving of a beautiful life anyways.
In spite of loss, in spite of grief, in spite of pain,
in spite of the darkest, coldest seasons tearing me to pieces –
I created a place where love and warmth
reaches us both
between these fence posts.

I wish I knew then what I know now -
You don't need to wait for flowers
when the garden grows within.

Broadcast Burning

What was buried down deep seems to be resurfacing.
I want wildness.
I crave a little chaos,
and need to break free from the monotony.
Something inside me has known for some time now
that change is coming.
My spirit,
chomping at the bit to sprint into the unknown.

What if going crazy is exactly what's necessary?

I stare out the window of my soul and watch the world go by.
Am I even a participant?
Once I'm done conforming
I wonder where I'll fit.
I wonder what life would look like
if I turned my back on it.
I wonder who I'd be
if I stopped being who I'm supposed to be.

What if I stopped settling for the scraps of status quo?
What if I binged and indulged?
What if I was irresponsible and reckless,
just for a second?
And started exploring everything eccentric within me...

I want to take flight.
I want to burn red hot again.
I want to wake up somewhere new.
I want to pull myself out of the rut by my roots
and toss caution to the wind.
I want to feel butterflies again.
I'm not closing the curtain,
I'm ripping it off its rungs.

I'm burning down dead growth
so that new life sees more of the sun.

Tied Like Garland

Something divine must be guiding me.
The way I'm being beckoned and led like the tide.
I dive deep into the crystal blue waters
and listen as the ocean speaks.

The greatest version of me,
nourished in aqua marine.
When you flow freely with belief and trust,
everything surrounding you seems serendipitous.
Life blossoms beautifully even in darkness, like the Tiare Maori.
Nothing is a mistake.
Every misstep a necessary one,
always taken at the right time and place.

My spirit returns home to passion and purpose.
With no obstacle too large to overcome.
I follow my heart faithfully,
with the universe in my favor
and no fear of the future.
This moment is all I have.
So, I cherish it.
I sink my teeth into it.
I wrap my arms around it.
I hold it loose enough so that it breathes effortlessly.
Tight enough that it's felt.

Freedom is knowing what's meant for you can never be stopped,
and what isn't,
must be released.
The sun sets,
the stars shine,
and life reminds us once again
that *we* are the magic we've been waiting on.

Rose Hips & Pith

I planted a rose garden in your honor.
Proof that sharp, painful things
also grow when watered.
The price of loss is peace.
I'm still learning who I am without you here,
while memories and *what-ifs* continue resurfacing.

Some nights, I forget you're gone.
Your presence keeps me company.
But I want to be free from grief.
I want to catch my breath and step into the sun again.
I need a new season.
One where heartbreak isn't raining down in heavy sheets.
I want to grow gentle things
that don't leave scars behind.
I want the air around me light,
perfumed sweet.

So much of the love I know bears thorns,
so I reach for it carefully.
I notice new growth in places you once called home.
Life goes on without you.
And without the pieces of me
that needed to be buried.

I planted a rose garden in your honor.
Proof that the things we can't let go of
becomes what never leaves us.
They grow roots within our hearts
and become a part of everything we are.
I walk through this garden
and see beauty blossoming in places
I thought would remain dark.

Don't Let Her Down pt. 2

Fall for a woman who doesn't need you.
One who has rebuilt herself from nothing, more than once,
with her own two hands.
One who is delicate like fire,
who could scorch earth
or warm your soul.
Fall for a woman who isn't afraid to burn for what she believes in,
and refuses to force
what isn't meant to be.
Fall for a woman who lights up when impassioned,
who still romanticizes life,
and is awed by the beauty of the moon.
Fall for a woman who isn't afraid of who she's becoming,
and still expects the best of everything.
One who refuses to settle,
and will challenge you to grow in ways you never knew.
Fall for a woman who is so loyal,
so faithful and determined,
that there's no room in her life
for anyone who isn't.
Fall for a woman who sees your pain and imperfections
as something to pour her love into.
One who accepts people for what they show her,
not what they promise or claim.
Fall for a woman who values her time so much
she won't waste it anywhere it isn't appreciated.
Fall for someone who will inspire greatness in you,
and who moves you in the direction of your dreams.

When you find her, be there entirely, bravely,
wholeheartedly.
Give her your hands,
your energy, patience, and attention.
And show her there is no place safer
than the place right beside you.
Then, no matter what,
  don't let her down.

Lift Him Up Pt. 2

Fall for a man who's strong enough to be humble,
and humble enough
to be soft.
One who actively looks for ways to be uplifting,
who understands how to lead,
and prides himself on promises kept.
Fall for a man who isn't above romancing you.
One who isn't afraid to get creative with his affection.
Who knows when your fire needs safeguarding,
and when it needs stoking.
Fall for a man who sees time shared together as something sacred,
valuable, and worthy of his attentiveness.
One whose smile brings peace.
One whose arms widely embrace,
with shoulders to carry the load,
and hands that are both protective and gentle.
Fall for a man whose words and actions are aligned,
who walks with discipline and high values.
Fall for a man who sees his shortcomings clearly
and rises to the standards his family deserves.
One who loves you openly, loudly, freely, easily.
Who never takes for granted how fragile and brief this life is.
Who understands that what gets watered
grows,
and that your heart never goes neglected.
Fall for his faithfulness, his transparency,
his thoughtfulness,
and the way he shapes the world around you.

When you find him,
fall all the way, and let him know
it's safe to do the same.
Then, no matter what,
be the very first person
to always lift him up.

The Waiting Pain

It's all different now. Without you here.
I replay all my favorite memories
like a reel of faded film.
In my mind, you're always smiling.
We're always happy.
You were the backdrop to so much of what I love about life
that celebrations and special occasions
are now just reminders of your absence.

People tell me that it will get easier.
Which I take to mean
breaking will soon come more naturally.
They tell me to just give it time.
But how do I explain that I'm waiting for a Spring
which will never arrive?
I wait to feel warmth in Winter's throat.
I wait for any sort of sign
that you're still here in spirit.
I wait to let go.
I wait to hold on.
I wait.
A part of me wants to skip ahead to the end
just so I can see you again.
But the other part of me
longs to be strong again.
And use the time I have here
to make you proud.
I want to carry you like a flame
and light others' candles with it.
Even when it hurts, and I'm alone,
I want to take the flowers you planted inside me
and spread them wildly,
with anyone in need.

I'm sorry I'm still weak.
I know you'd only want the best for me,
but I'm not sure what that looks like
or means, exactly,
without you.

I wait....

All I have is time...

and that's what hurts the most.

Sunshine

Despite the great risk, I choose love.
I choose to believe in impossibilities.
I listen to my intuition,
and trust what it's telling me.
We are not accidents.
We are not mistakes.
My vulnerability is my greatest strength.
My weaknesses are windows I hope we look through
and see one another.
All that matters to me now is the journey.
I want to appreciate everywhere I am.
Each step is taken for the first time.
My feet touch down gently atop new ground.
I wriggle my toes into the dirt and, my God,
it's great to be awake.
I will never have this moment again,
so, let's make it magical.
Let's *be* sunshine.
Let's walk each other home.
Let's trust the timing of life.
Let's appreciate the nuances of one another.
Let's accept honesty in energy.
Let's throw all our pieces in a pile
and take whatever's needed.

You see,
to experience life to the fullest,
we must die a little along the way.
Breaking is the prerequisite.
Healing is the gift you give yourself,
for which others benefit.
Let's celebrate what it took *for* us,
and *from* us,
to be here together.
We've come so far that we must be miracles.

My Hero, My World

My mother will have a hard time hearing this.
She'll roll her eyes when I say she's heroic.

You see,
my mother is so humble she doesn't know she's a mountain.
And that her strength is my strength.
My mother pours out so much love,
never knowing she's an ocean.
We all jump and swim and play in these waters,
and it's all because of her.
Her light shines on us, warms us,
gives and sustains life,
yet it never dawns on her that she's the sun.

My mother is as beautiful as she is modest.
As powerful as she is gentle.
My mother is magical,
the place we run to for answers,
and she doesn't realize that she's a forest.
My mother is everything I admire.
Everything I aspire to be more of.
Filled with pride,
yet never boasts or brags.
My mother is the loveliest person I've ever known.

She'll roll her eyes when I say she's heroic,
but she's the reason I know the word "love"
at all.
I see the entire world in her.
And what I hope for most
is that one day
she sees it, too.

Believe In Us

It's your fault for stirring my soul awake.
For setting fire to my spirit.
This version of me -
the happiest one I've ever been -
is your doing.
You've loved me so perfectly
that I learned how to love myself properly.
Now there's only you and I,
walking down unknown roads.

Maybe fear gets in the way.
Makes something clear and obvious
turn opaque.
We question our own capabilities.
Are we ready for something we weren't even expecting?
Are we even deserving of peace?

But you should know that when I think of us,
I only feel euphoric.
All I see is forever,
inside the glow of a home all our own.
You aren't just a part of my day,
you're like watching the sunrise.
You aren't just someone who crosses my mind,
you occupy my heart.
Something was missing before you.
Not just a vacant space beside me,
but a void within.
You entered my world effortlessly
and filled it with color.
You opened doors I kept bolted closed,
and light flooded back in.

I believe in us.
So, please, remember this -
We can be certain of one another
even when we're unsure of the steps.

Both Are Me

I crave a gentle life.
I know what hell looks like already.
More harsh lessons aren't necessary.
Give me soft evenings, sweet as chocolate.
Nights worn like wool.
Let's laugh till we're in tears,
alongside those who make loving us look easy.
I want to breathe in the air
of everywhere I once dreamt of making memories.
Though my hardships have shaped me,
in beautiful and painful ways I will forever be grateful for,
I want my days to be full and affectionate.
I want to be formless,
someone who flows and moves without worry.
Some days I'm water.
Others, I'm lava.
Both are real.
Both are me.
All versions of me are honest and necessary.

Who I am is safe when respected.

I'd rather be a great friend to a few
than an acquaintance to many.
I'd rather be widely accepting
than widely accepted.
I want to be the one who others know is safe to turn to.
I want to be the person who I needed all those years ago.
There's gentility within me that wasn't always there.
It grew from heinous places.
Cold, callous, remorseful places.
My softness is my greatest strength.
To not be hardened by the very things meant to break you,
that's what I'm most proud of.
Now, everyone near me gets my light.
This way we all shine.

Homecoming

Hidden within my own brokenness
were all the pieces needed.
I found trust in myself,
after losing it in others.
I found peace
in places of abandonment.
And an abundance of pride
waiting on the other side
of humility.
It took stillness to move me forward.
Letting go of dead weight made space for new life.
Pain lent me perspective.

I've come too far to look backwards.
My light reflects off a past
I no longer reside in.
The journey was discovery,
and even when wayward,
I was always worthy.

Life is a grand adventure unfolding before me,
and I'm reveling in my own revealing.
The further I go,
the more it feels like I'm just beginning.
My healing was a homecoming.
And in the end,
all the trials were trails
leading me back to myself.

Love Against All Odds

I refuse to live my life in fear.
Never again will I cower at another's thunder,
as if I'm not a hurricane myself.
Never again will I bite my tongue
because some can't stand the taste
of my truth.
Never again will I be wrought with doubt,
reduced by someone else's beliefs.
No, it will be peace and decency I display.
Not wounds and scar tissue.
I will not be summed up by my adversities.

Love against all odds,
will be my core,
my heart,
my identity.

How easy it would be to grow cynical,
after everything.
How easy it would be to turn malicious
and become the very things
that once threatened me.
I could grow cold and blame my distress
on an unfair world.
Instead,
I will be the tree whose roots run deep enough
to withstand unwieldy winds.
I will not turn bitter.
I will not break.
I will bear and share the fruits
of a spirit that refused to grow poisonous.

Even my defiance will be beautiful.
What I leave behind
will be something as strong
as it is sweet.

Spanish Moss

They say nothing is permanent.
Yet, so much of you remains with me.
Maybe the *only* thing which lasts forever
are feelings.
Speaking of you in the past tense is difficult
while still sensing your presence.
It's not an empty space standing in your place.
There are a million emotions morphing
and ever-changing.
Grief comes and goes
just as often as appreciation does.
I know how lucky I am
to have had you in my life.

What's difficult is not knowing
what to do with it now.
Who am I without you here?
Where does my path take me?

So much of me was wrapped in us,
that now I'm left in tatters.
Shreds of you cling to me
like Spanish moss.
I've come to appreciate
the way it drapes my days.

It's not all sadness in your place.
There's also a lot of life.
There's joy in our memories.
Comfort in recollection.
Faith in knowing I'll find my way.

Like a piece of parchment that's been balled up,
I smooth it out the best I can.
And then write what's left of my story atop every crease.
I'll make us proud.
It'll be worth reading.

Believe You

Believe you.
Listen to your essence.
Trust your truth - the gentle nudge,
those subtle gut feelings are instincts.

There will be times you'll want to run.
You'll seek and hide in places
where no one can find you but yourself.
Your aloneness, too, is a gift.
Closing doors around you
so that you may enter new ones within.
You are vast,
and uncharted.

How sad it would be to go a lifetime without having discovered
everything rare and valuable about yourself.
Walking your own roads as a stranger.
Believe you.
Turn over every boulder and find your awe again.
Don't be afraid.
Adversity is the night sky,
and your successes the stars atop them.
The mind binges
on what the heart is starved for.
Don't feed it doubt.
The stability you needed back then,
now exists within.
You are a mountain.
The love you once waited on,
grows from you like wild vines.
Being alone is never lonely
when your own company isn't a burden.
Look how light fills empty spaces
and what you made of yourself.
Believe you.

How Could I Not?

To accept yourself is an act of defiance.
The world prefers you fixed atop a potter's wheel -
malleable and reformed.
Something soft and impressionable.

The world prefers me meek and unsure.
But I see perfection in my reflection.
How could I not find this body of mine divine,
housing a soul so full of life and love.
How could I not find pride
in what I did to survive?
I crossed every bridge meant for me
without malice,
the best way I knew how to.
How could I not value what's left of myself?
It took a lot of hurt,
a lot of work,
to find beauty in places most can't see.
Healing happened once I owned my mistakes,
and they no longer owned me.

What are wings without resistance?
What's necessary to fly is never a fault.
All these deterrents and frictions
become prerequisites.
Clouds in cotton candy skies
I now soar through,

How could I not fly?
How could I not rise?

The River Alone

Sometimes the strongest people
were never given any other choice.
They're so accustomed to doing it alone
that letting go takes time.
Their hands and arms strained
from holding it all together tightly.
Their ribs, like a dam,
keep all that's in their heart
from bursting out of them.

Let her love rage like a river and pour forth.
Let her fists unclench and her arms slacken.
Let her soften and flow freely.
Respect the way she rises and falls,
bends, and crests.
It's taken a lifetime to get here.
Long enough to know there's no time to waste.
If it doesn't stir her excitedly,
or calm her peacefully,
let it drift by untouched.

Being strong every second of every season
is exhausting.
She's proven her self-reliance.
Yet she craves someone brave.
Stand steady in her waters
or remain on the banks where it's safe.
When you possess everything needed for happiness,
you learn that emptiness is a person
and never a place.

J. Raymond

The Same Ground

I once believed that making others happy might fix me.
Maybe if I made you smile, I'd find my own.
Maybe if you lit up when I entered a room,
I'd forget these dark ones I'm trapped inside.
Maybe if I was everything you needed,
I'd become everything I needed.

My first steps were on eggshells, toeing lines,
taken quietly enough to hopefully go unnoticed.
I grew atop cracked glass, afraid to run.
When all you know is being broken and used,
the idea of being whole again seems impossible.
I had to rip my roots out from dead earth and replant myself.
One-by-one I plucked out painful pieces.
Hurt I'd learned to live with.
Little by little I started healing and forgiving.

I didn't find my light overnight.
Compassion and confidence grew so slowly you couldn't notice it.
Each demon demanded to be dealt with,
and I did so afraid.
The hardest part of fighting for your life is what happens after deciding to.
They don't talk about how far peace and happiness are from hell.
I had to give myself all the things
others stole from me.
I had to sow seeds of tenderness in places that only knew pain.
I had to find the laugh I lost long ago
and be my safekeeper.

There are flowers where
there were once horrors,
and not everyone will understand,
but gratitude grows out of the same ground
tragedies are buried in.

Witness A Sunset

With every step, I unraveled.
A little more of me revealed
the further I went.

My heart, it turns out,
is both the strongest and weakest thing about me.
The way it bends and breaks and mends again.
I'm so wildly hopeful,
and I should know better but
I've yet to witness a sunset that wasn't worth chasing.
I've learned that my greatest failings
held the seeds of my biggest blessings.
I've learned that starting over
is sometimes a step forward.
I've learned when to let silence speak for me,
and that I'll roar for good reason.

I've got a long way to go,
though I'm always exactly where I'm supposed to be -
    finding peace in uncertainty.
The storms are part of my story.
Necessary to my journey.
I feel my old life wilting like weeds inside me,
while everything meant to survive thrives.
I'm not afraid of decay.
Like wildflowers, I open.
I grow.
There's beauty in my becoming.

We Can

I can tell you that I've wanted to die at times.

And I know I'm not the only one
who's plunged their trembling hands into cold bedrock
begging to hit bottom,
only to find it goes deeper.
At the end of my rope wasn't hope,
nor silver-lined light,
or even laughter.
There was only me standing there alone,
wrapped in survival that wasn't as comforting
as I thought it'd be.

Sometimes, the strength we find
leaves scars behind.
More thorns than floral.
Sometimes, you make it through
to the other side
with your pride ripped to shreds.
The dirt beneath your nails
serves as a reminder
of the hells you once called home.

I'm alive, but it isn't always glittery.
I'm alive, but there are times
I still look over my shoulder
and recount the wreckage.
I'm alive, but nobody prepares you
for how lonesome these roads will feel.
I can tell you that despite the darkness,
despite the wounds still healing,
despite a heart that's sometimes too tired
to try,
I'm grateful to be alive.
I'm grateful when I'm the color gray.
I'm grateful when my smile seems impossible
and sunlight seems miles away.

Peace knocks at the same doors I've kept locked and closed,
and I'm learning to let it in.
I'm learning to welcome it into a home
that's only known the opposite.
If you're ever tired of being strong, stop by.
We don't have to pretend to be intact.

We can break together.

Where I Go

Maybe I'm more hunter than I realized.
No longer one to sit and wait for life's flames to reach me.
I start fires now.
I sink my teeth into the mysterious
and indulge.

Passion goes where I go.

I won't settle for tepid or timid.
I won't accept the monotonous.
Give me haphazard adventures
and nights I'll never forget.
I deserve a love story for the ages.
Something red-hot and alive.
I won't be robbed of my fevered pleasure.
I want my guttural laughter,
and combustible experiences.

I will run from those who make life
less flavorful.
I will run towards all things hair-raising.
I will run alongside everyone effervescent.
I will run.
Because I've stood statuesque long enough.
I will run.
Because life is too short to count sheep.
I will run.
Because I'm more of a wolf than I realized.
I will run.

Lost Often

Please know, I'm not letting go.
My heart is still shaken,
though I'm getting through.
You'll never need remembering,
because I haven't forgotten you.
You're always nearby.
Kept close enough to feel and hear.

I guess those who leave behind a lot of light
also cast the longest shadows.

It sounds strange,
but grief is welcomed company some nights.
You meant so many different things
to so many different people.
The sound of your name
no longer cuts me open.
So I bring you up often,
hoping to discover another color
in which to paint you in.
Every story shared becomes another facet
for which light shines through.
I gather recollections
and see angles of you I never knew.
In the end, love is your legacy.

Your smile waits around the corner and greets us
when needed most.
I get lost often.
Even new memories are usually made
with you in mind.
I think to myself, "*You'd love this*",
and that little piece of me I thought was empty
is replaced with your presence.

For a moment,
I pretend I'm whole again.

Tempest

You're fine.
Say it again.
Until those two words reach your limbs.
Look in the mirror.
Ignore the tired in your eyes.
Implore yourself to smile.
Don't cry.
You're fine.
Get dressed.
Go be perfect.
Go be incredible.
Go be the friend your friends deserve.
Go be everything you're in need of.
Try again.
Try harder.
Don't quit.
You're fine.
Remember better days.
Disappear in them.
Come back stronger.
Stop complaining.
You're fine.
Be happy. Be happy. Be happy.
Be ashamed for not being happier.
Pull yourself out of it.
Find your footing.
Find your dreams.
You're fine.
Look for the light.
Be the light.
Work harder.
Work more.
Work.
Laugh, despite that sinking feeling.
Swallow the knot in your throat.
Step over the pit in your stomach.
It's not your fault that it's your fault.
It's ok to not be ok,
but hurry up and be ok.
You're fine.
Say it again.

Say it until you hate it.
Say it until you can't stand the taste of it.
Say it until there's no air left in your lungs.
Say it until you cough on your own exhaustion.
Say it one final time,
then swear to never say it again.

Don't leave the raging tempests within you untouched.
Let the heavy rain soak your burnt-out frame.
Stand still and beg for the lighting strike.
Feel all of life profusely.
Learn the rough weather you're made of,
until you love the storm you are.

Meet Me Here

Please let these words be a bridge between us.
Each one a steppingstone of sorts,
bringing you and I back together
whenever needed most.

Since the day you were born, you have meant everything.
Your life became my world.
Your heartbeat and breath became my own
from the very first second.
So much time will pile up between then
and whenever you read this again.
That, too, is a gift.

There are things I wish I could go back
and do differently.
Moments I wish I could re-live.
Some, so perfect,
I'd give anything to experience again.
While others,
I'd revisit simply to be better for you.
On my worst days,
and through my longest nights,
please know this - you were loved.

Despite my faults,
the times I may have let us both down,
and when I fell short of being who you needed,
you were loved.
You were loved when I wasn't there for you.
You were loved while I was breaking.
You were loved when I had none left
for myself, even.
I've loved you unconditionally.
I've loved you imperfectly.
And today, please know this - you are loved.
And tomorrow, you will be loved.
Love does not erase mistakes.
It doesn't absolve us.
Though it can change us.

It can inspire us and lead us down roads
we'd never walk otherwise.

If ever you're unsure,
always remember this - you are loved.
If ever you are scared, alone, tired, beaten down or heartbroken,
always remember this - you are loved.
There has never been,
nor will there ever be,
a single moment of your life
where you are not loved completely.

If you ever need reminding, please,
meet me here.

Paper Angels

I collect pieces of where I came from
and bring them with me.
Every severed stitch and string
lie in piles at my feet.
Like tiny birds' nests and tumbleweeds,
reminders of what I've overcome.

With scissors gripped tightly,
I'll continue cutting myself free.
Not all at once.
Carefully, purposefully,
a little more each day,
separating burdens from the lessons learned.
I'll cut away the dead weight
and hate.
I'll cut out the darkest parts of my story
and make them paper angels.
I'll unfold in front of you,
and show you that the only way to open
is honestly.

I won't pretend it doesn't still hurt.
Sometimes wings don't grow before you hit the ground.
Let's remember the fall.
Let's compare the scars we share.
If you're still dressing old wounds, that's ok.
Blood doesn't bother me.
Maybe some of the stitches I keep
are the stitches you need.

Colors Of A Campfire

If there is power in pain,
I will find strength in places
that have only known hurt.
My beaten heart
beat back.
Whatever quit existed in me
was used as kindling.
My soul warmed.
My spirit ablaze.
I must be the byproduct of problems and persistence.
The panned gold left behind
after all the mud and muck has been mined.
My worth wasn't inherited.
It was discovered.
Earned and unearthed.

I won't hide the parts of my heart I fought to find.
I'll let them burn.
I'll let the smoke in my eyes and watch gratefully
as it billows high into the night sky.
Little signals, should we ever lose our way.
I'll let its scent embed into the fibers of my clothes
and memorize the colors of a campfire.
Every yellow-orange rolling into red.
Only my love will scorch earth.
I'm entirely amber.

There's no going back now.
My road is wide open and only goes forward.
When you see me,
just know the torch lighting my way
comes from the same tamed flame
that once kept me at bay.

I Love You Means

We'll lose track of the number of times
"I love you"
leaves our lips.
Some will be flung flippantly over our shoulders
as we rush into the day
and out the door.
Others will waft whispery and exhausted
as we're drifting asleep.
We'll speak them passionately,
and we'll speak them passively.
We'll say it without thinking.
We'll say it before hanging up the phone.
We'll say it to celebrate.
We'll say it to soothe.

As the years go by, those three words
will be passed back and forth between us
thousands upon thousands of times.
They'll be as familiar to our ears
as our own name is.
But know this - even as they hang in the air you and I share,
those words, to me,
will never be weightless.
They will be full, though never heavy.
Carrying within them a million emotions,
infinite reasons.
I love you means peace.
I love you means your smile saves me.
I love you means magic.
I love you means never forgetting.
I love you means forever.
No matter how we speak it,
"I love you"
will mean *everything*.

Terrarium

My walls are decorated with all my favorite photographs.
Hanging plants and flowers from my ribs,
like the rungs of a ladder.
Fresh air climbs up to my lungs.

It's so beautiful here it takes my breath away.

Butterflies' flit by,
brushing excitement against my insides.
Milkweed and Bergamot grow wildly in bunches,
a bouquet of life.
Bees drink from brightly bursting colors
that look like fireworks suspended in the sky.

I'm happy to be home now that I've made it my own.

A version of me as a child runs by breezily,
free-spirited and without shame,
hopscotch-skipping atop my heart.
I'm safe here, all alone.
I catch my breath
and use it for laughter instead.
Look at this life I built from scratch,
with my bare hands.
The afternoon sun shines through my skylight eyes
as the windows of my soul are thrown open nice and wide.
This body is mine,
  I'll keep it graciously.

Surely, winter is over,
and I'm finally Spring.

J. Raymond

A Single Feather

See, the basement of our soul is not to be avoided.
You have been here before.
We are reconstructed from catastrophes.
We are reassembled wide-eyed in darkness.
We are nothing without our failings.
Our greatest strengths,
the very things we are most proud of,
are not what comes naturally.
We wouldn't waste dreams on flying,
if not for the risk of falling.

Find your foundation.
Find your essence.
Find your verity.
Peel back the painful layers
and pen a love story over vellum.
Find faith in a single feather.
Then find another.
And another.
And fashion them together into a pair of wings
that were always meant to be made,
not grown.
And once you've gathered enough strength,
leave this lowly place.
Leave it without angst.
Leave it without shame.
Leave this place in peace.

Crumble into dust, rubble, and debris.
Sink to your weary knees and bleed.

You're not falling apart,
you're becoming.

I Hope

I hope the holes in your heart fill with peace.
I hope you forgive those who aimed their pains at you.
I hope you don't blame yourself
for what was meant to be temporary.
I hope you love the company you keep.
I hope you keep the company you love.
I hope you only hurt for good reason.
I hope you still see how beautiful this all is.
I hope anger is fleeting.
I hope joy is long-lasting and deep.
I hope you laugh often
alongside those who stick around.
I hope every embrace is full.
I hope you know you're deserving of good things.
I hope you are always exactly where you're meant to be.
I hope those plans you laid
grow limbs and bear fruits.
I hope you find contentment in the way everything unfolds.
I hope you soothe whatever still ails you.
I hope you become the bridge to better days.
I hope you fall madly in love
with these moments.
I hope you are proud of what
you walked away from.
I hope you never look back.
I hope you find excitment in the present.
I hope you discover the power in your purpose.
I hope you hold onto hope
and I hope you never let go of your greatness.

Old Lows, New Highs

How cruel, that both the high and low points of life
can stem from the same person.
The greatest and worst blessing and curse.
Dreams and nightmares
with a common denominator.
The poison and antidote alike.
You'll enjoy breathtaking views together -
from mountaintops they'll later push you off.
And your broken heart won't be enough.
They'll break your spirit with it.
Like a knife in the wind,
cutting you out
with hardly any resistance.
Almost as if you never existed.

You'll wonder how the tides of someone you trusted
could turn so abruptly.
You'll wonder what more you could have done
if everything wasn't enough.
You'll wonder why you bother with someone
who stopped caring long ago.
You'll wonder.
And maybe more than anything,
you'll learn.

You'll learn that what hurts the worst
becomes what's for the best.
You'll learn that abandonment
is where you discover yourself.
Sometimes, the future we once imagined
is snatched from our grasp
so that fate may replace it with gifts.

Remember,
the love we seek cannot exist
where less is accepted.
Them leaving was never a loss.

Flourishing

Oh, how I love the way my heart opens -
expectations without attachment.
Holding onto my ideals
while allowing perspectives to shift.
I'm always full.
Waxing and waning
until the old me is eclipsed.
I'm in my unfazed phase.
Unbothered and unafraid.
Endings blend into beginnings.
I swear,
I've come so far to just be starting.
One long flowering.
Everything, all along
were lessons awaiting receipt.
There's no disappointment.
There's no disbelief.
There's nothing that can even alarm me anymore.
I'll find beauty in impurity.
My dark sides are as alive as the light.
I thrive in rayless places.
I won't house the hurt.
My soul is no derelict home.

I'll tend all the way out
to my edges and boundaries,
until there are gardens in my peripheries.
Look at my love flourishing,
reaching where I once couldn't even see.

Nearly There Now

Healing, it turns out,
is more difficult than hurting.
Pain and decay,
I know.
I understand it.
It's not difficult to wrap your head around
the very thing you're entangled in.
I've spilled good blood
chasing bad love.
Tossed and turned alongside the coldest burden.
Grew so close to blame
that we became one and the same.
Even my happiness felt infected.
Something accompanied with guilt.
Remorse coursed through my veins.

It's hard to understand,
but when all you know is the prick of the thorn
and never the rose,
agony becomes its own kind of comfort.

I chose my alleyways and backroads.
Constructed homes in heartless places.
Stood stubbornly beside the broken remains
of my own disdain.

Have you ever hurt too much to cry?
Your body withholding the weeping
your soul so desperately needs.
If I seem tender now
it's only because of how life has beaten me.

I say all that to say this -
just beyond the devastation
exists freedom in its purest form.
A land where nothing threatening lurks.
Whatever comes next

comes with reverence.
The days awaiting you,
just past the bend and break ahead,
are golden lit and cordial.

You're nearly there now.

You Are Not Alone

Leave. Find any way out. Plan your escape.
They will not stop.
They will never change.
The abuse will grow more violent.
It will only get worse.
Leave.
With whatever you can.
As soon as you can.
However you can.
Do not stay here.
This is not a home.
This is no safe place.
Leave.
Love is not a punishment.
This isn't your fault.
You are not to blame.
Leave.
Leave kicking and screaming if you must.
Muster up every ounce of bravery and courage and run.
The sun will never rise here.
Kindness will only be applied
over injuries they cause.
They spit band-aid lies
and weaponize empathy.
Leave.
Your heart does not belong to monsters.
Do not let them feast on it.
Do not give them any more of your soul.
Leave.
Rebuild from scratch.
You can.
You will.
This is not the end of your story.
Fight.
Flee.
Leave.
Do not accept this broken fate.
Do not let them bury you alive.
There is no excusing their fists.
There is no forgiving their viciousness.
They deserve no tears from you.

They deserve no explanation,
no reason,
no leniency.
Leave.
Leave them where they belong.
Let them rip themselves to pieces.
Let them tear themselves apart.
Let them rot.
Leave them empty and pathetic.
This is not love. This is not love.
This is not love.
Understand this - you are not weak.
It's your strength they're most afraid of.

Leave.

Whatever's Left

There's not enough left of me.
I'm ash and scraps.
More odds than ends.
And you deserve far more than anyone's remnants.
I'm something mangled,
pretending to be mended.

But you should know,
the only time I ever feel anything close to whole
is when I catch a glimpse of myself through your eyes.
You're the reason I've made it this far.
You're the reason I held on.

As I disintegrated,
you gave me someplace to sift through the pieces.
   Then you sifted with me.
As I was losing whatever trust I had left,
you collected and kept it stowed away.
   Then showed me where to place it.

Maybe I'll never be intact again.
Maybe I'll keep the keys to these locks hidden and buried,
just to keep myself from reopening.
Maybe I'm afraid of losing what's been salvaged.
Honestly,
you've shown me a love so great,
so unwavering,
that I'm not even sure my heart is comparable.
I can't be who you need me to be.
I can't give you what's left of me
when there's still so much missing.

Happiness awaits us both.
Soon, someone will love you in all the ways
I never could.
You deserve a world I can only step aside for.
Please know,
I look forward to the pain of that day.

Like Oceans

There are days the distance between us seems too much.
Like oceans,
the space and time apart
goes on and on,
further than my eyes can see.
The horizon blurs into blue forevers.
But what do you do,
other than wait for what's meant to be?
What sense is there in counting days
or biding time?
What's the point in hurting over something
that's only unfolding naturally.
Exactly as intended.
As destiny designed.
What will be
requires no force,
no urging,
no coaxing.
And like oceans,
we float to keep from being crushed.
We let the thing itself
carry us,
without worry of beginnings and endings.
It's all new.
The view, ever-changing.
Maybe it's best if we just drift a bit.
See where it takes us.
See if these waves bring us to the same place.
Either way,
it's all been beautiful.
You've been my favorite part of life.

Just Look

All her life she's been invalidated.
Minimized and made to feel less than.
One-too-many times taken advantage of
by the very people she'd do anything for.
Used and fed upon.
Shown and then settled for
the lowliest versions of love.

This is how one is reduced....
Slowly punched down and shrunk over time,
until the bright, audacious life they once envisioned
is replaced with something quaint.
Something unremarkable.

Yet, her dreams haven't ceased.
There's still fire and desires ignited inside her.
There's wide-open road and wild adventure ahead of her.
There's nothing left behind worth going back for.
Leave the hurt.
Leave the remorse.
It's not luck which carried you through.

If you need proof,
look how far you've made it on your own.
If you've misplaced your pride,
remember that you went through it all alone.
If you're still unsure of your strength,
just look how you grew
after everything they tried to take.

In the end, there is you -
the only validation you'll ever need.

Hope Climbs

It begins so slowly you hardly notice.
Joy shows up in subtle ways.
Smiles come more often and easily.
There's suddenly new energy in your eyes.
Little things are noticed again,
appreciated again.
You're healing.
Each day, a little stronger.
A little more resilient.
Hope climbs back in
through the same cracks that
left you broken.
You catch your breath again.
You get lost in someone again.
The sun rises
and your spirit lifts again.

This is what we do.
We endure.
We come back.
We rebuild ourselves.
From disheartening pain
we evolve into someone even more loving,
more determined,
more embracing and accepting.
We become who we deserved all along.

The losses I once thought were too large to overcome
are a part of the foundation I now stand upon.
Everything hurtful became helpful.
I found the fullness of faith
in empty places.

Maybe the views are so wildly beautiful
because of everything gutting I had to go through.
If love can grow from sadness,
I'll let light in through my damage.

Love Letters

All this time I've beaten myself up
when what was needed most
was love.
I've yelled at myself to fight,
when I should've been whispering forgiveness.
I don't even care whose fault it is anymore.
Who am I to judge,
with all these regrets and negligence?
There's no untangling me.
I've got to string together a life
we might be proud of,
despite the knots.
Despite the tension.
Despite my fraying.

The only ones left
are the ones staying to see me make it.
They deserve better than love letters.

I wonder what life would look like
if I wasn't so afraid whenever it went right.
If I stopped slitting my own throat
and calling it a smile.
If I saw myself as more than my mistakes,
or as anyone other than who I was
on my worst days.
I'm trying like hell to give wings to the parts of my heart
that have only ever fallen apart.
I'm trying to let go of who I had to be
to even make it this far.

Still Searching

Softness takes time.
My heart, a ripening fruit,
aging like port wine -
too sweet to swallow.
I wasn't always so kind to myself.
Pride climbed the vine so slowly
I thought it might not ever arrive.
Today,
the sun seems to shine brighter
wherever I stand up for myself.
The warmth was waiting on me,
while I was waiting on it.
I've identified the blame.
Rid myself of resentment.
Stopped pouring myself into places
laden with pain,
and rebuilt where I felt full.
Those closest,
the ones making it all worthwhile,
are all the motivation I need.
What I find beautiful now,
is simple, though not easy -
loyalty
friendship
family
compassion
peace
this moment

I'm still searching for where I belong,
accepting that everywhere and nowhere at all
might be the answer.
But learning to love myself along the way
has been the greatest discovery I've ever made.

J. Raymond

The Ride

If there is peace on this journey,
thus far,
much of it has eluded me.
With strong, spent legs
   I keep going.
I keep running,
clutching what's left of this worn out heart,
wondering how far one must go
before they find somewhere serene,
somewhere
they're meant to be.

I've collected lessons like scars
and memories
like stars,
and so much of who I am today
is because of the person
seen from afar.

My road has rarely been easy.
So few steps taken over smooth surfaces.
Still, it's the unevenness of it all
which steadies me now.
It's knowing that,
despite tumultuous times
and treacherous seasons,
I,
myself,
have endured.
I,
myself,
walk forward led by light.

If there is love on this journey,
it's because I carry it within me.
I'll find peace in persevering.
I'll find happiness within my own grit.
I'll look back on my losses and smile....
so many life-altering mile markers made into victories
because I refused to quit.

Litmus

Love must be tested for it to be strengthened.
Trust is earned in time.
Intimacy grows slowly,
and is always evolving.
Bonds are forged in fire,
and hearts atrophy without effort.

What I'm trying to say
is that I'm not going anywhere.

Everything great in this world
must be fought for and earned,
and I know that we can be great.
More than anything,
I believe in us.
Our journey won't always be clear.
There will be rough roads and weather
we'll travel through together.
And despite our best intentions,
we will fail.
We'll hurt one another.
We'll feel lost at times.

And it's from these very places love grows.
Not from mountaintops,
but from valleys.
Not where the ground is easy
and well worn,
but from where most are too afraid
to venture to.

Real love lives in the fight.
In the stress and inconvenience of life,
and heals two people at once.
Where we go from here
is entirely up to us.

So Long

In time,
she'd trade the cage for blue skies.
Throw herself to the open roads
and make life an adventure again.
Her only regret will be that she stayed so long.

The most important lessons
usually come wrapped in a tragic package.
They bruise us to the bone.
Clipping our wings
and turning us into a feeble thing.

In time,
she'd make her life her own.
Taking back the reins
others had grabbed ahold of,
and bringing warmth into her home.

Caring for yourself feels foreign
when all you know is repairing others.
Loving yourself always seems selfish
to those who don't view you as a priority.
In time,
she'd find freedom in falling apart.
Breaking in ways that strengthen the spirit.
Few things hold a person back more than loyalty misplaced.

Hold your own heart.
It'll never be valued by someone unfit.
There's worth in your rarity
and power in your individuality.
Play. Laugh. Run wild like a child.
Never lose your good nature.
Go discover all those curiosities
and don't fear going off path.
Maybe you were never meant to
find your way back.

Little Corner Full

The toll trauma takes on the soul
is measured not in sadness,
but in aloneness.
We call it "*space*",
when in reality,
it's pain that's confined us to islands.
The depth in connecting
becomes a danger we distance from.

For her,
the breaking point
was the turning point.
The hard right
after everything went wrong.
She's still punishing herself over what others did.
But hate will never satisfy a heart
that's starved for love.
You can't punish yourself back into place.
Don't slam the book closed
because of past chapters.
Your story is still unfolding,
and it needs light.
Set free the fireflies
shining brightly within your tightly cupped hands.
You are not your tragedies.
You are not your failings.

How beautiful it would be,
to make that little corner of the world
you were backed into
somewhere welcoming.
How brave it would be,
to look fear in the eyes
and for it to see all your love staring back,
wildly.

The Sweetest Company

I'll keep the space between
what could have been
and
what was meant to happen
somewhere empty of sadness and regret.
Instead of obsessing over endings
I'll focus on moments worth remembering
and fill those spaces with life.

I've drifted atop this narrow river for some time now,
yet I sense the ocean approaching.
A future sprawls out in directions I've never been
and I'm excited for depth,
and the changing of tides,
and the crashing of waves.
I want to be drunk on sunlight
and for me to be
the sweetest company kept.

Please understand,
I find life far too beautiful to be weighed down
with regret.
My heart isn't heavy.
I don't agonize over outcomes.
I celebrate the journey.
And the way one moment branches out
into the infinite.
Everything, again,
  is possible.
But I'll start with not settling.
I'll begin with a spark.
and build my own fires.
If passion is best unfettered
mine will be wild and free.
And whatever is awaiting me
won't be waiting much longer.

There are promises I've made with myself
that I intend to keep.

Just Ask

Ask,
and she'll tell you how a heart can learn to heal itself.
She'll show you how the same cracks allowing light in
also cast shadows you'll want to hide in.

Ask,
and she'll show you how a smile can mask the hurt.
She'll explain how the surface hardens
as the spirit softens.

Ask,
and she'll explain why the greatest gift one can give themselves
is acceptance.
She'll show you how the holes
shot through her soul
are shaped in such a way
that only love can fill them.

Ask,
and she'll tell you how she lost herself
attempting to be and please
everyone else.
She'll show you,
home is where a gypsy soul goes wayward.

Maybe freedom is forgiveness.
Maybe peace exists in your own embrace.
Maybe pride is survival.
And,
maybe,
what matters most
is the way she makes something beautiful from the ruins.
How she'll turn obstacles into advantages,

and grow through the very things meant to be crushing.

We deserve only what we accept.
And her heart learned to expect a miracle.

Ask,
and she'll show you how she became one.

Don't Hurt Yourself

What hurts is when asking for anything
feels like asking for "too much".
What hurts is giving everything to people
who leave you in pieces.
What hurts is putting yourself
back together again
without losing your worth.
What hurts is how good I am at healing.
What hurts is time.
What hurts is when others would ask how I'm doing,
I'd lie and say "fine".
What hurts is when they know the truth.
What hurts is that I have nothing to show
for the things I fought for.
What hurts is feeling used.
What hurts is not trusting myself.
What hurts is the way I never let myself get too excited about anything
anymore.
What hurts is keeping my heart quiet
when all it wants is to leap and sing.

What hurts is that I waited for an apology
you thought was undeserving.
What hurts is how long I waited.
What hurts is how the ones hurting you
will try and convince you they aren't.
What hurts is that I nearly believed them.

And now that I'm through hurting,
one thing is evident:
no amount of pain will turn me into someone who inflicts it.
Hurting me is going to hurt you
a lot more
than it hurts me.

Right On Time

It's funny,
I once hated them for the way they left me.
Now I just shake my head for staying so long.
Time cuts in both directions,
but the river only flows one way – forward.
An ocean, washing lessons and people ashore.

But you...
I would choose every version of you,
in every lifetime.
Over and over and over again.

There were many days I felt it was "too late".
Like I was destined to be left behind.
Maybe my dreams had passed me by,
the windows of opportunity
all closed and locked tight.
And other days
I felt as if I had plenty of time,
all of it in the world.
So much I couldn't hold it all.
I'd watch as it slipped through my fingers,
spilled out of my hands.
I rushed nothing.
I ran nowhere.

But I see now, it was all leading me here –
to you.
Every person was preparing me.
Honing and tuning me just right.

It's funny, the way I believed they broke me.
They convinced me I was ruined.
Unlovable.
Someone to pass through,
never somewhere to grow roots.
It's clear to me now – those not meant for us
can never love us properly.
I tried so hard to pull love
from the wrong people.
I tried to will myself into being

who they needed me to be.
I know better now than to fight for something
that can't be forced or coerced.
All that pain was the universe saying,
"Not this one".

I just wasn't listening.

It's amazing that every person who hurt me
was only bringing me to you.
I'm sorry it took me so long to be right on time.

8.9.24

A letter to my expecting wife:

These are our final few days alone together. Our life, our world, is about to be very different. So, I just wanted to take a moment for us, to slow down and catch our breath. To pause and reflect.

You, my love, are the embodiment of awe. Watching you has inspired me in ways I didn't know were possible. To watch you, over the last nine months, is to know the true meaning of strength. How you've grown physically pales in comparison to how you've grown emotionally. I won't pretend to know the pain and discomfort that comes with creating life. I won't pretend to comprehend the fear and anxiety associated with motherhood. But what I know, with absolute certainty, is that you've handled it all with grace and bravery. You are, quite literally, becoming the mother you needed as a little girl and I'm so proud of you. Look what our love did. Look what came from never giving up and finding our way to one another.

But, I need you to know something, while it's just you and I. While it's still quiet in our home and we're well rested. Before the upheaval and wildness sets in. You, my love, will always be my priority. I will be by your side every step of the way. Do not be afraid. With every fiber of my being, down to my marrow, I will love you. I will love you in such a way that our daughter will never wonder what the word means. She'll see the depth of my love lived out loud, every single day.

I will remember these days forever. Resting my hand on your beautiful belly, feeling her kick. Feeling your skin stretched tight like a drum, home to a heartbeat. Half mine, half yours. You've redefined the meaning of "Us" in the most beautiful way, and I'm honored to be your husband. Thank you for making me a father. Thank you for being the woman, friend, and mother you are. Now, when I think of my future, I think only of my girls.

My Girl

It's all different now...

Just like they said it would be.

Little girl, you've changed me completely.
How surreal that the purpose and point
of my life,
all along,
was you.

One day, when you're older,
I'll tell you how it felt to hold you
for the first time.
How every word I'd ever learned
abandoned me,
so that I could finally understand what it's like to feel something
I could never describe.
I'll tell you how the first time
you opened your eyes, you opened mine.
And when you fell asleep on my chest,
every single heavy, hurtful thing I'd been carrying inside me
was finally set free.
A dandelion blown by a baby's breath.

One day, when you're older,
I'll tell you how the day I met you
was the day I met me.
Existing deep within was someone warm and loving
that only your hands could reach.
Only your love could touch.
I'll tell you how you taught me unconditional.
I'll explain how you made me brave.
How I knew at that moment there was nothing in this world
I wouldn't do for you.
I'll spend forever bringing you the moon.
Bringing you the stars and sky.

One day, when you're older,
I'll tell you how it felt to write these words,
knowing your life
saved mine.

J. Raymond

CONTRIBUTOR LIST
(Not In Order)

Janell S. – Boca Raton, FL
Gini T. – Montgomery, AL
Amanda R. – Nashville, TN
Andrea M. – Austin, TX
Anonymous – Pattaya, Thailand
Courtney R. – Lubbock, TX
Diana A. – Pomona, CA
Dana C. – Kirkland, WA
Ramona M. – Glendale, AZ
Heather M. – Salt Lake City, UT
Jessica S. – St. Louis, MO
Penny D. – Burr Ridge, IL
Deb D. – Hurst, TX
Charlotte Q. – Richmond, KY
Melissa G. – Bradenton, FL
Victoria B. – Montreal, Canada
Rose M. – Township of Clinton, MI
Christina O. – Ocala, FL
Georgia D. – Wales, UK
Yvette M. – Bay Area, CA
Jackie F. – Rocklin, CA
Julie B. – Wixom, MI
Sheena L. – Tujunga, CA
Samantha M. – Shakopee, MN
Jade G. – Bluffton, IN
Darlene C. – Hopewell, NY
Kurt M. – Jefferson, GA
Eduardo H. – El Paso, TX
Kyla T. – Jefferson City, MO
Sarah L. – Queensland, Australia
Emily R. – Germany
Irene R. – Phoenix, AZ
Ericka A. – Lakewood, CA
Suzanne N. – Gilbert, AZ
Jennifer S. – Johnston, IA

Sammy & AJ – Goodrich, MI
Melissa S. – Easton, PA
Ludia S. – Riva, MD
Daniel R. – Worcester, MA
Lindsey D. – Eugene, OR
Laurie T. – Provo, UT
Erin W. – Keizer, OR
Andrea B. – Warwick, RI
Alexandra H. – Ontario, Canada
Erin L. – Urbana, OH
Amanda M. – United Kingdom
Megan B. – St. Louis, MO
Anonymous – New York, NY
Jules B. – Northland, New Zealand
Tria B. – Claremont, CA
Hayley J. – Victoria, Australia
Michelle R. – Marshfield, MA
Brittany G. – Blackjack, MO
Carrie P. & Mari-Beth
Kersten J. – Louisville, KY
Suzie S. for Aliyah – Cleveland, OH
Shannon S. – Dayton, OH
Laura B. – Hendersonville, TN
Nichole H. – Alberta, Canada
Leann B. – Madera, CA
Rebecca S. – Central, LA
Sybille H. – Germany
Mamta B. – Bangkok, Thailand
Stacey W. – Old Saybrook, CT
John W. – Birmingham, AL
Liz D. – Indianapolis, IN
Cathy M. – Smithtown, NY
Brittany M. – Vancouver, Canada
Casey F. – Minnesota
Essie L. – Englewood, NJ
Christina P. – Port St. Lucie, FL
Loretta L. – Virginia
Sue J. – Queensland, Australia
Melissa H. – Marion, NC
Mairead T. – Leinster, Ireland
Jessica L. – Vero Beach, FL
JeriAnn S. – Eastsound, WA

Kyle K. – Alberta, Canada
Tony M. – Maryland
Nicola G.
Vashti W. – New South Wales, Australia
Ashlee H. – Columbus, GA
Mariette B. – Netherlands
Lindsey D. – Eugene, OR
Lisa W. – Indiana
Lori P. – Englewood, FL
Devon G. – Templeton, CA
Katrina B. – Puerto Rico
Anita M. – Chicago, IL
Aaron R. – United Kingdom
Janet K. – Salem, MA
Michelle T. – Henderson, NV
Beth F. – Aurora, CO
Millie N. – Newark, NJ
Stephanie G. – Mesa, AZ
Sharon L. – Durham, NC
Sean B. – Chesapeake, VA
Fallon R. – Fresno, CA
Brianne H. – Albuquerque, NM
Ryan E. – Chula Vista, CA
Tatiana R. – Garland, TX
Mariah V. – Tampa, FL
Anonymous – Philippines
Ali A. – Denver, CO
Lisa E. – Wichita, KS
Catherine W. – Buffalo, NY
Derrick F. – Canada
Hannah P. – Madison, WI
Lori S. – Palmdale, CA
Nancy A. – Little Rock, AR

J. Raymond

OTHER BOOKS BY J. RAYMOND

SPADES
LET HER RUN
CONCRETE MUSIC
YELLOW #5
LUSH
SPADES/LET HER RUN: HARDCOVER SPECIAL EDITION
THE KINDRED PROJECT

FOR INFORMATION ON CUSTOM POEMS,
SIGNED BOOKS,
TYPED POETRY AND OTHER ARTWORK,
VISIT:

WWW.JRAYMONDWRITING.COM

JRAYMONDWRITING@GMAIL.COM

ABOUT THE AUTHOR

Husband.
Father.
Observer.
Thinker.
Writer.

"I don't have any problem understanding why people flunk out of college or quit their jobs or cheat on each other or break the law or spray-paint walls. A little bit outside of things is where some people feel each other. We do it to replace the frame of family. We do it to erase and remake our origins in their own images. To say, I too was here." – Lidia Yuknavitch,
The Chronology of Water

Made in the USA
Middletown, DE
04 January 2026

24822398R00117